BRIDGING

THOUGHTS

A compilation of psychology related published
articles imbued with Filipino contexts

Dr. Aggie Carson-Arenas

Volume II

To

Allen, Arjohn & Amer

Acknowledgment

Thanks to the publisher, particularly the editor-in-chief of the *Philippine Daily Inquirer*, US Bureau for granting permission to include copyrighted articles in this collection; and for the joy of bridging thoughts... the ephemeral fame with readers.

Specially to the researchers, experts, authors and contributors quoted or cited; as well as those whose names are not meritoriously mentioned.

Copyright Credit

Preface

Bridging Thoughts (Volume II) is a compilation of psychology related original articles published in the United States (*Inquirer*, US Bureau); a few imbued with Filipino contexts.

Each piece attempts to present, expound and simplify (demystify?) psychological concepts pivoted on current events, issues and technologies -- often tinged with privy advocacy.

A kibitzer friend reminds us that technology is bridging our thoughts into a boundless collective connectivity, which we *then;* could not have imagined.

Please, let us bridge our thoughts some more...

Aggie

Contents

Yesterday's sorcery, today's psychiatry?

By: Dr. Aggie Carson-Arenas
Columnist, Inquirer, U.S. Bureau. August 04, 2021

"The most beautiful thing we can experience is the mysterious. It is the true source of all Art and Science," according to Albert Einstein. Despite that, *all* sciences evolved from magico-religious ideas, quips a skeptic-kibitzer friend.

Our ancestors based their cures and theories almost entirely on superstitions and magic, as attested to by historical writings. It was *science* that led the revolution against medieval thought.

The earliest "healers," whom we refer to today as "health providers" (a.k.a. physicians or doctors) were often practicing occultists who tussled with occult causes of diseases.

History depicts that early medical sciences — including the science of the mind — embodied a number of magic practices. Curiously, these "health practitioners" were not prosecuted though we know *today*, that they were dabbling in magic arts and occultism.

This is perhaps why Hippocratic practice, or medicine and psychiatry, as we understand them today, became the *first* "sciences" – due to the urgency to rectify such practices.

Master

Evolutionary scientists estimate that humans had existed a million years ago, yet man appears to have had only several thousand years of written human history! The *oldest* ancient Egyptian papyrus discovered in 2013 is estimated to be a mere 4,500 years old. Papyrus was used in ancient times as a writing surface.

This means healing in all its forms, as proof of biomedical or biopsychological writings, are historically, relatively *new*. Our knowledge of the full nature of the sciences is still in its infancy in spite of all the vigorously conducted investigations, studies and theories formulated.

Our civilization probably improved by a thousand-fold, yet the world as a whole seems to remain like a vast unexplored entity, awaiting discovery and rediscovery because when the sciences obtain an answer; the answer only reveals more unknown beyond.

Evolution *in* the universe is science in action that never stops; it only pauses, unfolds, and refolds further. Science is a perpetual cyclic phenomenon that no man can have absolute control of, quips an evolutionist-kibitzer friend.

Record

Our concepts of all sciences are constantly changing due to results of novel studies and new *advanced technologies*. Contemporary scientists are thus beginning to disprove or validate long-held notions.

The opt-quoted title, "*Absence of evidence is not evidence of absence*" by Drs. Altman, D. G. and Bland, J. M. seems to convey to current scientific realm that, "The *truth* in their results is barely enough... the *advancing technology* (newest) will rile, roil and reek, or let them reap new accreting dimensions," quips another reductionist-kibitzer friend.

It is estimated that new knowledge is generated at the fantastic rate of almost a million pages per minute; the Covid vaccine is one latest proof; new elements are being discovered. The acceleration of computer capacity starting from kilobytes (KB) is now in *exabyte* (EB) — one primal commercial hard drive is priced at US$72,545 — will amaze, astound and alarm the mind.

Artificial intelligence (AI) is creating, interpreting and leading information technology into seemingly mystical dimensions; almost akin to jumping into another unknown-dimension-portal, quips a *portal-*obsessed kibitzer friend.

Guttenberg

Humans' thirst for knowledge is the driving force in seeking to satisfy his curiosity of his own nature and his arts. The vessel that truly quenching this thirst for knowledge was the discovery of the printing press, quips a magus-kibitzer friend.

The invention of the printing press was the enlightening transition from medieval period to modern science. This facilitated the first means of recording, studying (analyzing) and interpreting on a larger scale *human thoughts*, quips again this kibitzer friend.

These are the fundamental components of scientific pursuits necessary to profess objectivity, verifiability, validity, dissemination and continuity for other future researchers to examine, refute or expound to arrive at the *truth*, added this kibitzer friend again.

Guttenberg commercialized printing in 1450, which accelerated the dissemination of information concretely. The impact of *written words* upon medieval healing was dynamic, yet not without resistance from the "earliest (medieval) healers." The popularity of written words threatened traditional beliefs and practices.

The new breed of self-proclaimed "knowledgeable experts" met their predecessors with considerable hostility, calling them occultists and sorcerers for refusing to conform to their then-thought "scientific" tenets and methodologies.

Cryptic

The teachings of "medieval healing" were once contained and guarded — *cryptically*. The techniques and methodologies were handed down from one generation to the next through actual rituals, ceremonies, word-of-mouth devoid of written records. Healers intentionally kept their "system" secret.

The "system" was practiced as a well-guarded secret by a select few thus remained the great 'mystique' for centuries. However, this 'mystique' was later demystified and *exposed* through written words (writings).

Writing knowledge (recording) was the beginning of bridging thoughts among men. The bridging has expanded through *advanced technology* today. However, an anti-Qanon kibitzer friend quips, "Has technology really succeeded in eliminating the beliefs, rituals and practices of the medieval era?"

When modern science falters, men regardless of creed, race, political affiliation, apparently tend to fall back easily to occult belief. Empirical studies show that folk medicine or occult healings are still common today, quips an urban-legend advocate kibitzer friend.

When the cause of an ailment is unclear or seems to strike without reason (like Covid?), even a modern man tends to attribute it to an "invisible entity" taking over. Many find it easy to revert to medieval practices, conspiracy theories or malinger Qanon syndromes.

Breed

As early as 1425 a *new breed* of "healers" called themselves "physicians," wrote Maple E., an English folklorist. These organized *physicians* attempted to disentangle their newly acquired status as "new healers" from sorcery and witchcraft. They launched violent attacks against their sorcerer-precursors.

They thought themselves "learned experts," establishing the *English Guild of Physicians*. The Guild started to define and refine their own tenets and precepts as "science." They were trying to turn medieval medicine into organized, formal and "scientific" knowledge.

This was probably the formal beginning of the *allopathic* practice of medicine, a mechanistic theory of diseases and treatments one learns through standardized formal study, observation, practice and experimentation. This is the foundation of today's modern medicine.

Future

Some beliefs are as widespread as ever, having withstood the test of time. Some wax and wane insidiously at certain epochs; some are adapted into contemporary lexicon, like the *anti-vaxxer*.

Was witchcraft of yesterday the psychiatry of today? What will become of psychiatry tomorrow, quips a nosy, melioristic-kibitzer friend.

Moreover, the futurist Arthur C. Clarke might have clued us in with a sort of sweet clarification or Aufklärung when, more than a half century ago, he observed that any sufficiently *advanced technology* is indistinguishable from *magic*.

There's the rub; there's the folly. A Qanon-syndrome-afflicted enabler could yet help foment other conspiracy theories.

Quo Vadis, my enabling one?

Delegitimizing the experts

By Dr. Aggie Carson-Arenas
Columnist, Inquirer, US Bureau, August 10, 2020

"Today, everyone knows everything: with only a quick trip through WebMD or Wikipedia, average citizens believe themselves to be on an equal intellectual footing with doctors and diplomats," writes Dr. T. Nichols in his pre-Covid book, *The Death of Expertise.*

This Oprah Winfrey Show, started in 1986, comes to mind. The show seemed to demystify "unknown" (a.k.a. rare) psychological (and other) disorders by presenting the case and cure, often with a live afflicted being on television.

Viewers got a lot of information about the disorder and treatment. Some viewers probably felt blessedly wiser — many unwittingly making themselves armchair experts — gasping at the misfortune and treatment of others, quips one of my analytical kibitzer friends. Many got out of their snuggest armchair.

The audience got a lot of information. But did they get the "knowledge," the *dynamism* behind *the* patient, *the* disorder, and *the* treatment? To be a doctor (or an expert) is a challengingly arduous and expensive paperchase, quips my other doctorate kibitzer friend.

"We (Americans) long ago became a narcissistic nation whose citizens believe they can become competent in almost any subject by watching enough television and spending enough time on the internet," adds Dr. Nichols, an adjunct professor at the Harvard Extension School and a prolific author.

Distinct

'Information' and 'knowledge' are distinct: "Information is extremely cheap to produce… knowledge is incredibly expensive to produce," averred Dr. J. Donovan, a social scientist and director of the Technology and Social Change Research Project at the Harvard Kennedy School.

One can easily share or get information freely from myriad platforms freely offered by tech-companies. You can bridge your unabridged thoughts with the world. However, this may change now that the scrutiny of Congress is inching towards the "Four Titans of Technology," so we are told.

Moreover, Dr. Nichols reminds us that, "Technology and increasing levels of education have exposed people to more information than ever before. These societal gains, however, have also helped fuel a surge in narcissistic and misguided intellectual egalitarianism that has crippled informed debates on any number of issues."

It seems everyone knowing everything. The *truth* is thus negated or distorted; at its worst, it is sometimes intentionally delegitimized through misinformation.

Does reaching into your pocket to "google" information mean grasping the "*knowledge*," the essence behind the topic? rhetorically inquired my doctorate kibitzer friend.

Delegitimize

Before the current political zeitgeist, which we now must endure, we were relying on medical providers and scientists for *good* information. But everybody agrees no one is truly infallible; expert failures are real and happen every day. In fact, "Some reject expertise because of the previous 'failures' of experts. This is always one of the reflexive explanations for the refusal to listen to the educated and experienced," again stated Dr. Nichols.

The danger, bluntly stated by Dr. Nichols, is when ordinary citizens believe that no one knows more than anyone else, democratic institutions themselves are in danger of falling either to populism or to technocracy or a combination of both.

A person in authority, like a president turned "enabler,' is a millionfold more influential and toxic, who can wield quasi-cultish power, quips an apolitical kibitzer friend. People who reject expertise because they believe they are smart and clued into the mistakes of experts will accept the words of an "enabler."

Reason

There must be a reason why many Americans think they are smarter than experts. Paradoxically, wrote Dr. Nichols, the increasingly democratic dissemination of information, rather than produce an educated public has instead created an army of ill-informed and angry citizens who denounce intellectual achievement.

Are we all afflicted with the *Dunning-Kruger Effect*? This is a cognitive (mental) bias in which one is apt to assess his or her cognitive ability as greater than it truly is. One often overestimates himself as "knowledgeable" when, in fact, he lacks real (factual) knowledge.

"Because we are unaware of our deficiencies, we generally assume that we are not deficient, in keeping with the tendency of us to choose what we think is the most reasonable and optimal option," according to

Drs. D. Dunning and J. Kruger. Is the Dunning-Kruger Effect being boosted by *technology in your pocket* or by a toxic *enabler-in-authority*?

Charles Darwin more than two centuries ago aptly summed this up: "Ignorance more frequently begets confidence than does knowledge."

Using Hypnosis In Dentistry*

By Dr. Aggie Carson-Arenas
Columnist, Inquirer, US Bureau, April 22, 2021

Who would believe that a tooth extraction could be an awe-inspiring experience. Using *hypnodontia* can be a positive experience that you will never forget. It becomes even more unbelievably awesome when the tooth extraction is done *without* an iota of anesthesia.

Hypnodontia, more currently known as *hypnodontics*, is one of the more objective manifestations of hypnotic application: observing an excruciating pain zapped by hypnosuggestion.

I am not a dentist, but a long time ago, I was a young enthusiastic novice starting to practice hypnosis – I had just received a certificate in hypnotherapy. I was a junior in pre-med school at the time, and I got into this exciting dental process by twist of fate.

The experience was a milestone that gave me the confidence during this critical phase of learning the practical applications of hypnosis. Without this experience, I might have been discouraged and lost interest as most beginners do. That was several decades ago; now, I am proud to announce that I have authored an introductory manual on hypnotherapy as proof of my endless enthusiasm about hypnosis.

Before sharing this awe-inspiring experience, let us first consider a brief overview of hypnodontia.

Root

Hypnodontics is the use of hypnosuggestion in dentistry as a means of relaxing tense patients, relieving anxiety, reinforcing, or replacing anesthesia, and correcting such habits as bruxism (clenching or grinding the teeth and jaw). Hypnodontics simply means the dental application of hypnosis to allay fear and anxiety and to alleviate pain. It is also applicable for all procedures from tooth extraction to root canal.

One study conducted almost half a century ago suggests that the incidence of dental phobia is at 6.9% of the general population and 16% in school-age children. This data are likely much reduced today due to sophisticated instrumentation and state-of-the-art dental practice. However, studies today show that many patients put off going to the dentist until the pain or dental problem becomes intolerable. This is often due to phobic reactions or anxiety and fear.

The first reported practice of hypnodontics was in 1836 when a French physician, Jean-Victor Oudet, applied *hypnoanesthesia* in a dental extraction; this procedure then was identified with "mesmerism." Ribaud and Kiaro from France followed in 1847 when they did a similar procedure with a jaw tumor excision.

Hypnodontia is relatively easy to apply to a highly susceptible individual. In fact, the Scoring System for Inducing Depth Hypnosis designed by LeCron-Bourdeux (which I dubbed the 'Hypnometro') is only between Depth 33 (Complete anesthesia) and Depth 34 (Posthypnotic anesthesia) out of the possible 100, both under Deep and Somnambulistic Trance Level.

Process

The experience that I had with hypnodontia (with a dentist) is really the benchmark of why my enthusiasm with hypnosis has endured. I enjoyed sharing this experience with my psychology students whenever we discussed the autonomic nervous system (ANS). However, I never hypnotized a single student during my entire professorial career, except in suitable milieus (lectures or seminars) where I was doing hypnotic demonstration. Here is the story:

One of my cousins L, about 12 years old, got an appointment for a tooth extraction. I volunteered to drive him to the dentist office. Upon reaching the place, L became so apprehensive that he refused to go into the dentist office! I tried to cajole him but to no avail. Then, thinking this could be an opportune time to practice 'hypnotic power' on him, I casually asked, "Would you like to be hypnotized?"

"Yes!" L replied unhesitatingly. He agreed to enter the office, so I could discuss the matter with his dentist. After a few cordial greetings, I brought out the question, "Doctor... have you ever heard of 'hypnodontia'?" The answer was an emphatic yet affable, "No."

Fortunately, he allowed me to provide him with a half-hour lecture on hypnosis (luckily it was a not busy day for this dentist). The dentist was convinced. "How do we start," was like music to my ears. My response was, "We just need to follow the flow. I will first hypnotize L, of course..."

The truth of the matter is I was not sure of what to expect, or of the outcome; using the word "flow" was purely metaphoric. I was busy trying to muster consciously what my subconscious mind had imbibed from the handful of research that I had read about hypnodontia, which was really not much!

The hypnotic induction with L went smoothly. The dentist was impressed. I felt good myself.

Unbeknown to the dentist, I already hypnotized L many times before and found him extremely susceptible. I did a 'negative hallucination' test with ease. In the process, I also gave him a posthypnotic "cue word" for easier and faster hypnotic induction in the future. Therefore, in my calculation, L was indeed hypnotically ready.

Although this was actually my first attempt at hypnodontia, I seriously kept mum, intentionally evading the words "experiment," or "first time" with the dentist. I did not want the dentist losing confidence in me at this point. However, I would have told him the truth if he had asked.

Induction was quick due to the *pre-suggested* posthypnotic cue previously given to L. I repeated several times the word "ticniv," a kind of anagram for the Latin word "vincit" meaning, "conquer." I sensed the dentist's curiousness as to what this mystic-sounding word meant; however, he did not ask. I was fine with that; spared me the time of discussing *posthypnotic phenomena*, which could have led into another lecture session.

When in my calculation L was in a hypnotic level, I hoped (and prayed) he was, the dentist interrupted and said, "What's next…?" Without hesitation I said, "Scrape the gum…to expose the tooth." (To validate my calculation… or identify that L was not at the level I suspected he was…).

There was no pain-reaction whatsoever manifested by L! I literally felt my heart jump with excitement; and then I had some apprehension: Excited because I believe, we achieved the right hypnotic level, and apprehensive about the prospect of L waking up unexpectedly. The dentist and I were both awestricken. I tried not to show my excitement, or the fear; instead, I tried exuding a calm confidence.

"What's next...?" asked the dentist again.... "Poke on the bad tooth..." I spoke. He did a few times. We observed no adverse response from L. "What's next...?" the dentist asked again. "Pull the tooth out!" I replied with urgency. He did, while L remained in a seemingly pleasant state of sleep. The process was successful, and surprisingly there was less blood than usual (according to the doctor). The dentist was flabbergasted; and so was I.

Upon my dehypnotization of L, the doctor, addressing L, declared, "Done!" L, who seemed stupefied for a moment was checking out the bad tooth using his tongue. With disbelief painted all over his face, he uttered, "Oh!" We showed him the extracted tooth and then provided him a mirror to check for himself. The doctor glanced at me and quipped, "Magic!" "An actual objective manifestation of hypnotic power," was my reply, with a quiet sigh of relief.

Proof

The living proof of this experience still exists. My cousin L now lives in Northern California with his family, and he still remembers gleanings of this experience; and he loves to talk about it!

Of course, not everybody might be as hypnotic-susceptible as my cousin L might. Hypnodontics is a *selective* procedure: it is not for everyone. However, it could be highly effective with select dental clientele who are fearful, tense, nervous, or anxious before and during dental procedures.

Hypnodontics can also be one excellent alternative among hypnotic-susceptible individuals with anesthetic or drug intake issues or concerns. This clientele may represent a small minority in the population of an average dental practice; however, they often present the majority of problems the dentist encounters in his daily routine.

Finally, the final conclusion according to philosopher Bertrand Russell is that "We know very little, and yet it is astonishing that we know so much, and still more astonishing that so little knowledge can give us so much power."

Dare to refute that.

*Dr. Carson-Arenas is a certified hypnotherapist. This is a true experience which took place in the Philippines many years ago. Readers are warned that the real dental procedures and techniques presented were only "tolerated culturally" in the said country at the time. Dr. Carson-Arenas founded the Psi-Hypnosis Society Inquest (PSI), Inc. with a group of students from different universities in Manila to study paranormal psychology in the Philippines; probably one of the first registered with the SEC as a non-profit organization — Dr. Carson-Arenas still has the original SEC registration.

A mystifying (terrifying) mind 'trick'

By Dr. Aggie Carson-Arenas
Columnist, Inquirer, U.S. Bureau, June 29, 2021

> Do not go gentle into that good night.
> Rage, rage against the dying of the light.
> — Dylan Thomas

One morning in August, Dr. C came an extra several minutes earlier before his morning class. He sat down to read a couple of memos, sign documents, and write a memo… when suddenly he had the *sense* of not knowing where he was… nor what to do next!

Dr. C simply felt confused – detached from *everything*.

The feeling was inexplicably frightening. Dr. C stood up, gingerly, quietly paced the room like a cat in an unfamiliar place. He felt his whole existence faded with his dreams.

Is this it… what now… what will I do? These were the questions he remembered whirling inside around his head during those moments.

Dr. C sat down trying to breathe as normal as he can. He forced his eyes shut. Dr. C self-talked in his mind to "relax… relax… it will pass… you should know better… you are in control…." Dr. C attempted to keep his mind as blank as he could.

Yet the sensation of losing in touch persisted a few more minutes.

It was so alarming that Dr. C could hardly keep his mind blank hence opened his eyes. He was testing his equanimity; deciphering a reality check.

Dr. C was almost on the brink of panicking when suddenly the vague unquantifiable 'feeling' eschewed, vanished as sudden as it appeared! He felt relieved, hesitant but continued, finished writing the memo.

Suddenly, Dr. C remembered his morning class. Where are my lecture notes? The index cards were nestling on top of his stack of biopsychology books. He consciously scanned reviewing the notes for a few minutes, then went out his office.

Dr. C dejectedly attended his first morning class. However, after ending the lecture; he felt good and believed he was able to deliver the lesson well for that morning.

When Dr. C went back to his office, slumped into his swivel chair, closed his eyes thankful for being himself again – for being *aware* again.

Dr. C was no longer confused.

In his mind, Dr. C was rationalizing – or self-diagnosing: If indeed I lost my memory…how could I have presented the lesson well… I had no problem in my presentation. I know where I am… what I did…

Dr. C regained his composure. His confidence returning although tinged slightly with a feeling of trepidations. Could this be real?

This experience only took a few *rare* minutes, but it was the most alarming experience. Dr. C is still mystified – still frightened that this might happen again at any moment, at this very moment.

Dr. C made it through that day. However, before leaving the office with his staff gone, Dr. C made the briefest, solemnest prayer: "Thank You for giving me back my mind."

Driving home, a quote from Dr. Hering, E. popped into Dr. C's mind. Upon arriving home, he pulled one of the index cards file marked "Memory, Mind, Dr. Hering, E." to read:

> It seems, then, that we owe to memory almost all that we either have or are; that our ideas and conceptions are its work, and that our everyday perceptions, thought, and movement is derived from this source. Memory collects the countless phenomena of our existence into a single whole; and, as our bodies would be scattered into the dust of their component atoms if they were not held together by the attraction of matter, so our consciousness would be broken up into as many fragments as we had lived seconds but for the binding and unifying force of memory.

Moreover, a significant picture flashed too in Dr. C's memory remembering the picture of the human *brain* he clipped from a magazine when he was in high school. Meticulously, he framed the clip in a small, gilded picture frame after scribbling in bold letters these three words: "Where All Exist."

Epilogue

This phenomenological experience of Dr. C seems (maybe) 'demystified' by contemporary psychopathology identifying this as *transient global amnesia* or TGA. The Mayo Clinic and the APA Dictionary of Psychology define TGA as a sudden, temporary episode of memory loss occurring in the absence of any neurological abnormalities.

During a TGA episode, recollection of recent events simply vanishes; one cannot remember where he is or how he got there. However, one do remember who he is, and recognize the people he knows well, making this 'temporary' loss of memory disturbingly frightening.

Fortunately, TGA is rare, seemingly harmless and unlikely to happen again. Episodes are usually short-lived, and afterward one's memory returns unscathed. There are no bona fide precipitants of TGA; the specific causative agent or entity remains unidentified.

The cycle of a mystifying mind gently bemuses Dr. C with a sweet caveat some more.

Dr. C is an alter-ego friend of this author's biopsychologist kibitzer friend.

The power of lying

By Dr. Aggie Carson-Arenas
Columnist, Inquirer, US Bureau, March 25, 2020

Almost all patients tell some lies while in therapy, wrote Drs. Blanchard and Love in their book, *Secrets and Lies in Psychotherapy*. Lying is not only common, but also ubiquitous... it's inevitable in psychotherapy, noted Dr. Farber, a professor in the clinical psychology at Columbia University.

A client has the right to lie all he wants to his therapists although honest disclosure is at the heart of all psychotherapy; but if someone feels like he needs to lie, that may also be important, according to Dr. Blanchard, a clinical psychologist at New York University.

To a psychotherapy client, the *importance* may be based on "distress minimization," or acting happier than one (actually) feels, to not wanting to upset the therapist or be seen as a complainer, or to protecting himself from a painful realization of how sad things may actually be, again according to Dr. Blanchard.

Does this mean that when a client lies to a therapist, one lies only to himself? The content of one's lie is insignificant to everybody else except to himself whatever is the content or purpose of the lie. The act of lying changes nobody but himself. The ponderous effect is only burdened upon him, quips my behavioral-analyst kibitzer friend.

Would the same principle apply when the same psychotherapy client lies to people, caveat publicly?

Amoral

The rub is, when a client or anyone, especially someone with of higher-status, prevaricating to others bears pitfalls. The dangerous thing about lying is people don't understand how the act changes us, according to Dr. Ariely, a behavioral psychologist at Duke.

My honest-kibitzer friend quips, Most of us resent any suggestion that external influences determine our behavior; we see ourselves as free beings, as the originators of our own actions. Yet are we absolutely free-beings uninfluenced by a seemingly ethereal but insidious force, like a lie?

One study documented children lying as early as age two, suggesting lying is a developmental milestone requiring sophisticated planning, attention and the ability to see a situation from someone else's perspective, again according to Dr. Ariely. But for most people, lying gets mitigated as we develop a sense of morality and the ability to self-control.

We are, however, reminded that we are *born amoral*; our sense of morality we learned from the world is recursively anchored on the myriad predisposing elements in our brain, again quips my very honest-kibitzer friend.

Yet, If you give people multiple opportunities to lie for their own benefit, they start with little lies that get bigger and bigger over time, stated Dr. Sharot, a cognitive neuroscientist at University College London. What then constitutes a lie?

'Consciousness of falsity'

Lying occurs when a communicator wittingly intends to mislead others as contextualized in the oft-quoted notion by Dr. S. Bok — the moral question of whether you are lying or not is not settled by establishing the truth or falsity of what you say. To settle this question, we must know whether you intend your statement to mislead.

Thus, it is not sufficient that something is false for it to be a lie; it is the intent that distinguishes the lie, according to Ford, King, and Hollender in their study, *Lies and liars: Psychiatric aspects of prevarication.*

We are our own judges about our own honesty and that internal judge is what differentiates psychopaths and non-psychopaths, again according to Dr. Ariely. Akin in context, Ford, et al. suggested the "consciousness of falsity" in their study as to distinguish "normal" lies from pathological ones.

"Normal" is often thought of as a misnomer in psychology and is difficult to define; but "pathological" is that that persistent, compulsive tendency to tell lies out of proportion to any apparent achievable advantage. It is most common among individuals with personality disorder, who do not seem to understand the nature of a falsehood.

The American Psychological Association (APA) defines *pathological lying* as a clinical syndrome characterized by elaborate fabrications, usually concocted to impress others, to get out of an awkward situation, or to give the individual an ego boost. Unlike the fictions of confabulation, these fantasies are believed only momentarily and are dropped as soon as they are contradicted by evidence.

Typical examples are the tall tales told or acted out by people with antisocial personality disorder, histrionic, narcissistic, borderline, and compulsive personalities although the syndrome is also found among malingerers and individuals with factitious disorders, neuroses, and psychoses, so we are told.

Control

Dr. Langleben, a pioneer in lie detection study, contended that it is possible that lying is essentially harder than telling the truth, because to lie does not involve any *impulse control*: One had to have good impulse control to otherwise the truth comes out first.

The key point is that we need to exercise a system that oversees regulating and controlling our behaviors when we lie more than when we just say the truth, again according to Dr. Langleben who also pioneered employing *functional magnetic resonance imaging machine* (fMRI) in his deception study.

Three areas of the brain generally become more active during deception: the anterior cingulated cortex (monitor errors), the dorsal lateral prefrontal cortex (control behavior) and the parietal cortex (process sensory input). When the fMRI scans show more blood is flowing in these areas of the brain; this indicate that all sections are functioning solidly.

Integrating, and then analyzing fMRI pictures, Dr. Langleben concluded that lying increased blood flow in these key areas of the brain. Blood flow equates to lying, inferring lies are not created out of thin air. Dr. Langleben's study suggested that the brain must think of the truth, and then decide, which in a sense, does the opposite.

This was demonstrated in a study when an experimental cohort was instructed to express (lie) "the sky is green." Dr. Langleben proposed that the cohort's brain first thought about the typical color of the sky, which is generally blue before he decided to express the falsehood. That thought process was calculated by the fMRI scan.

Caveat

Lying has long been a part of everyday life. We could not get through the day without being deceptive. Yet, until recently, lying was almost entirely ignored by psychologists, leaving scientific discussion to ethicists and theologians, according to Dr. Saxe, a professor of psychology at Brandeis University.

Freud wrote next to nothing about deception; even the 1,500-page *Encyclopedia of Psychology*, published in 1984, mentioned lies only in a brief entry. However, as we delve deeper into the studies of deception, we are apt to recognize lying is a surprisingly common but complex phenomenon.

New breeds of "physiologic detectors" are emerging, prompted by the more sensitive brain-imaging techniques, reawakening interest in lie detection as demonstrated by the advent of new instruments such as the, Near Infrared Spectroscopy (NIRS), thermal imaging, fMRI, and the Brain Fingerprinting technologies.

Despite technological development, self-report data for the U.S. adult population indicate the average rate of lying is around 1.65 lies per day. On any given day, most lies are told by a small portion of the population, where nearly 6 out of 10 Americans claim to have told *no* lies at all, suggested in a study by Serota, et al. of Michigan University.

Finally, according to the physicist Niels Bohr, "There are trivial truths and great truths. The opposite of a trivial truth is plainly false. The opposite of a great truth is also true."

Refute that with your *alternative truth*.

An 'infodemic' is worsening the pandemic

By Dr. Aggie Carson-Arenas -
Columnist, Inquirer, US Bureau, July 08, 2020

After the infamous Bible-waving photo-op at Lafayette Park during which police forcibly removed hundreds of protesters, William Barr the Attorney General of the United States of America declared on national television that police used "… pepper balls… pepper spray is *not* a chemical irritant. It's *not* chemical."

"He (AG) never heard of 'OC spray'? My adolescent kibitzer-patient quizzically asked. *OCD*? "No, *oleoresin capsicum* silly, it's from pepper… must be irritating chemical, Google it," replied the 16-year-old. "I think my mom use it for cooking too," added the kid.

The Department of Justice chief, the US government's top lawyer, was simply being asinine, at least to a 16-year-old boy. The AG is an "*infodemic*" spreader, quipped again my also-media-savvy kibitzer patient.

Conspiracy

"'Infodemics' are an excessive amount of information about a problem, which makes it difficult to identify a solution," according to Dr. T. Adhanom, Director-General of the World Health Organization (WHO). The term was coined in 2003 in relation to the flood of information accompanying the SARS outbreak.

An infodemic can be a spread misinformation, disinformation and rumors, which from WHO's vantage point, pertains to a health emergency like the Covid-19.

Barr's "non-chemical" OC-spray is misinformation; connoting an implicit lie to cloak a political problem someone in the White House might consider an "emergency." "Infodemics can hamper an effective public health response and create confusion and distrust among people," added Dr. Adhanom, to which my older political kibitzer friend interpolated, "often rooted in conspiracy theories so prevalent relative to current pandemic issues."

Of conspiracy theories, M. Sullivan of the *Washington Post* wrote, "In his radio broadcast, Rush Limbaugh came to believe that vitamin C was a possible [Covid-19] remedy; the Chinese government created the virus in a lab; and that our government health agencies were exaggerating the dangers in the hope of damaging Trump politically."

Conspiracy theories are powerful, according to Dr. K. Starbird, an associate professor of Human Centered Design & Engineering at the University of Washington. "Unlike science, conspiracy theories are uncomplicated and explain a chaotic world in a way that gives the believer a feeling of control."

"When these 'theories' become embedded, however, they can be difficult to refute with evidence," added Dr. Starbird, whether or not the evidence is irrefutably proven by *scientific* evidence

Pernicious

One pernicious outcome: Many Americans are convinced that wearing a protective mask is ineffective, a symbol of left-leaning partisanship. This, despite National Institute of Allergy and Infectious Director Dr. Anthony Fauci's public advice that wearing a mask is an effective deterrent to the spread of coronavirus.

We are not just fighting an epidemic; we are fighting an infodemic, which spreads faster and more easily than the virus itself, expressed to Dr. Adhanom during a WHO gathering foreign policy and security experts in Munich, Germany in mid-February.

In February President Trump insisted, "We're going to be pretty soon at only five people. And we could be at just one or two people over the next short period of time... *It's going to disappear...*" After four months almost three million have been infected and 150,000 have died.

Cheap

"Information is extremely cheap to produce" while knowledge is expensive to produce, according to Dr. J. Donovan a social scientist and director of the Technology and Social Change Research Project at the Harvard Kennedy School. You don't need any evidence, you don't need any investigation, you don't need any methods to produce it; social media platforms are freely available.

"There's so much information, it's so chaotic, and we're denied our social routines for helping us make sense," according to Dr. N. Ellison, a professor of information at the University of Michigan. "And the tech itself is shaping the information and the ways we engage with it in a specific way."

Dr. Donovan stated bluntly, "The coronavirus and the accompanying deluge of misinformation have laid bare a truth about the Internet itself: The early notion that users could be both producers and consumers of information has turned platforms into information landfills, where people are forced to sift through increasingly dangerous garbage in the search for real information." Platforms, suggested Dr. Donovan, should move beyond moderating to curating information.

The coronavirus has provided an unprecedented opportunity for those who intend to benefit from spreading false information, according to Dr. Claire Wardle, co-founder and director of *First Draft*, an organization dedicated to tackling misinformation globally. The pandemic has also united fringe activists and conspiracy theorists around a common distrust of institutions like public health organizations and other government agencies, Dr. Wardle added.

Mythbuster

The WHO has created its own "mythbuster" to work with search and media companies like Facebook®, Google®, Pinterest®, Tencent®, Twitter®, TikTok®, and YouTube® to counter the Covid infodemic.

"Our common enemy is a virus, but our enemy is also a growing surge of misinformation. So, to overcome this virus, we need to urgently promote facts and science," explained WHO's Dr. Adhanom. "We also need to promote hope and solidarity over despair and division."

Self-tracking health data with 'wearables'- a brave new world

By Dr. Aggie Carson-Arenas
Columnist, Inquirer, US Bureau, December 28, 2020

McDonald's dumpsters in Las Vegas are currently installed with cameras and sensors to get better at determining *what's inside*, reported R. Crane of *CNN Business*. So far, it has processed over 80 million images from the 162,000 cameras according to Compology.

Compology is a recycling company based in San Francisco since 2013 applying *artificial intelligence* (AI) to monitor what's thrown into dumpsters to distinguish recyclable materials, like cardboard, from being contaminated by real junk, in order to segregate them as non-waste.

Our current "wearables" come to mind. According to an ad pitched by a wearables company, "Thanks to recent developments in consumer technology, it is now possible to see *inside your body* and to track vital health signals for yourself, in the comfort of your own home. It's like taking a free physical exam – at home, whenever you want!"

Moreover, "Scientists are starting to put 'brain' in dumb substances..." wrote Begley and Service as early as three decades ago in their piece, *Walls with Eyes*. The "transition" glasses you wear or the toy animal that "grows' in water clues us how far we have gone.

Can we truly see inside our body with a wearable, incredulously inquired my heretic-kibitzer friend? Do wearables hold some kind of *psychical* mystique?

Self-quantification

The human is a mere bevy of numbers, so is everything in life, my bio-physicist kibitzer friend quipped. "Everything you feel is physiologically expressed in the *proteome* and *meta*bolome" (denoting genome, cell, tissue and molecule interactions within a biological system), asserted Dr. H. Heine, researcher and founder of a bio-tech company in 2012.

Proteome and metabolome, which are observable, constitute us as human. This means that every substance, cell and energy in the body is measurable by instruments, reagents, and software. Thereby, the self is *quantifiable*, wrote my alter-ego kibitzer friend in, *From Know Thyself to Track Thyself* almost a decade ago.

"Self-tracking" was first proposed by G. Wolf and K. Kelly, editors of *Wired* magazines, in 2007. However, it was Dr. L. Smarr, a Nobel laureate, astrophysicist turned computer scientist, who started charting his bodily inputs and outputs in minute detail, revealing the true ecology of the *quantified self.*

Dr. Smarr, a decade ago started collecting information on everything—from how well he sleeps to the state of his poop. Dr. Smarr appeared to have concretized the dictum, "track thyself" by the methodology he initiated.

Self-quantifying is the 'self-tracking' of our own behaviors, physiology, genome, down into molecular activities. The primary goal: to search for harbingers of our current or future health conditions. Self-tracking devices became practical, inexpensive, and ubiquitous. Currently we call these *wearables*.

Behind

Today, we not only understand why and how organs functions, but also how and why molecules make these possible. All these we can record as *data* — all of which we can derive from self-quantifying instrumentation and/or with recorded medical information. All these "data" are processed with the aid of *algorithms* and AI technology.

Every wearable gadget basically "detects" physiologic activities of our autonomic nervous system (among others). This is "recorded" then converted into "'data" we can collectively call "biofeedback." *Biofeedback* was coined by N. Wiener who pioneered research during the 1970s when "algorithm" was not yet a buzzword.

Algorithm is simply an instructional schema(s) protocol for a specific task. "Algorithm is the soul of computer," declared in an article in the *National Geography*, Partner Content section in 2019; if so, artificial intelligence is its consciousness, explained my biophysicist kibitzer friend.

Upon "analyses" of data, the algorithm processes then presents "options' or best solutions or interventions ranging from elevated blood sugar and injecting the right dosage of medication, to alerting the specific provider. All recorded, synchronized and orchestrated of what is happening inside the body — all in real time.

Ninety four percent of US hospitals can now access and analyze electronic health records (EHR) of millions of patients for almost everything from blood pressure, nutrition, to effectiveness of specific treatments modality to the spread of infectious diseases, so we are told.

Because of the omnipresent computer software, every collected data or "feedback" are retrievable wirelessly, 24/7, anywhere and everywhere for interpretation, manipulation, or diagnosis. A wearable is akin to wedding ring worn by anyone married to medical issues, quipped my satirist kibitzer friend.

Tool

Biofeedback machine, the precursor of the wearable was intended as a training tool to "subdue" our physiological responses in order to "consciously train" the mind to transform these responses and achieve a certain level of "behavioral modification."

Knowing what is inside of us is crucial. The early detection of any anomaly in the body is always a salient crux for a timely diagnosis for treatment. The technology embedded into our wearables appears to be really speeding things up.

Perhaps when these truly become infallible, the precise drug will treat the precise virus strain identified by and through the precise apparatus. Medical conjuring will become no more, quipped my alter-ego kibitzer friend.

Is the Covid vaccine with 95% efficacy, which was created in nine months, proof enough? I wonder who would win in building the first kinder *Earth Elysium*?

Why racism is more than skin deep

By Dr. Aggie Carson-Arenas
Columnist, Inquirer, US Bureau, June 12, 2020

Is Tiger Woods an "African American? Or is he an "Asian American," or even a Native American, or Dutch? Mr. Woods' ancestry is 25 percent African, 25 percent Thai, 25 percent Chinese, and one-eight Native American and Dutch.

Nature does not cluster races in neatly defined categories. It is people, not nature that sometimes label individuals like Mr. Woods, according to Dr. D. Myers a world-renowned social psychologist and author, and chemistry magna cum laude.

In the context of the world, every race is a minority, added Myers. This means we are almost the same genetically speaking. We are mere hodgepodge of races making everyone equal but distinct at the same time, quips my faux-geneticist kibitzer friend.

In fact, it is estimated that non-Hispanic whites are only one-fifth of the world's population; this estimation was made more than a decade ago. It will be one-eighth within another half-century. This is based due to the mobility and migration during the past two centuries. Whether we like this or not, the world's races now intermingle, so we are told.

Does this intermingling rile the interracial relationships we are currently experiencing?

To molecular biology experts, one's skin color is a trivial human characteristic controlled by a minuscule genetic difference between races. Yet today 'color' seems to define an inexplicable halo causing so much racial prejudice or racism, quips again my kibitzer friend.

Is racism really… truly more than skin deep?

Boundaries

To label an individual like Mr. Woods apparently sets some kind of 'boundary.' Imagine labeling a million people antagonistically. This means creating subtly what many sociologists and social psychologists classify as the *ingroup-outgroup phenomenon* popularized by Dr. H. Tejfel, a Polish psychologist four decades ago.

As soon as boundaries are drawn around an 'outgroup' based on race for instance, an invisible cohesion is built among its individual members. This breed unilateral images of people *competing*. This concept is best reflected by the Olympic Games first started in 776 BCE. Tajfel reminds us that the personal self-esteem of each member increases following a *group* success.

This kind of ingroup-outgroup division, forewarned by Dr. K. Sun in 1993, provides the matrix for *biased thinking* and *prejudice*. 'Close-mindedness' is probably the third partner of 'biased thinking' and 'prejudice' to construct a robust triad-twin, quips again my kibitzer friend.

To 'categorize' people however has an adaptive function, according to Dr. G. Allport in his oft-quoted book, *The Nature of Prejudice*. The human mind must think with the aid of categories. Once formed, categories are the basis for normal prejudgment. We cannot possibly avoid the process. Orderly living depends on it, wrote Allport.

In other words, Allport was suggesting that this is necessary to reduce the vast complexity of our social world to manageable dimensions. When we place people in categories, we help make our life's adjustment speedy, smooth and consistent; to sustain order and minimize chaos.

However, simplifying through categorization readily leads to oversimplifying and consequently to distortion, writes Drs. P. G. Devine et al., in *Social Cognitive Impact on Social Psychology*; sometimes cloaked with prejudice.

Thinking in categories is the *prototype of prejudice*, again wrote Myers. And this 'prototype,' has been subjected to *intensive* study by social psychologists, which seems devoid of lucid results to date. There is the rub.

Prejudice

Man is not born prejudiced, prejudice is learned. Prejudice by its very nature denies individual human dignity and breaks the fundamental unity among people, ironically wrote Allport, in his oft-quoted book.

Prejudice is the way one thinks or feels about a particular person or group. This often serves as an affirmation of being part of an *ingroup* or an *outgroup*. Groups are usually biased in their perception of themselves and others. They are likely to attribute positive attributes to members of their own group than to those of an outgroup, so we are told again.

As a result, prejudice can give an individual a false sense of identity and self-worth. This initiates the tendency in him to discriminate against others, making himself feel more powerful and elevating his own self-esteem. Categorization and stereotyping also often offer a convenient scapegoat for an individual or group in dealing with issues.

Prejudice is generally a way of thinking or feeling towards others, while discrimination is the *acting* on that negative prejudice. Thus, when things go wrong, people are likely to assign more blame to a member of an outgroup than to a member of their own group meta-studies of prejudice reveal.

Empirical studies also show the greater the competition between the groups, the more these similarities and differences are accentuated. Group experiences also affect how people think and feel about themselves. As mentioned earlier, people show an increase in personal self-esteem following a group success according to Tajfel.

However, members whose self-esteem has been diminished by a group failure show an increase in prejudice, wrote J. P. Forgas & K. Fiedler, "*Us and Them: Mood Effects on Intergroup Discrimination*." Members of any group may be prejudiced against different races or ethnic groups without realizing it, according to P. G. Devine et al. in a study entitled, *Social Cognition*.

Cycle

To understand the nature of prejudice not only requires knowing what a prejudiced person thinks, but also of how he thinks. A clue to this understanding is found in study of *intolerance* specifically of the '*closed mind*' concept pioneered by Dr. M. Rokeach, a Polish American social psychologist as early as four decades ago.

A person deemed high in ethnic prejudice is rigid in his problem-solving behavior, thinking, and narrow in his understanding of subjects of vital interest to him. He is prone to make snap judgments, dislike ambiguous situations, and show distorted memory of momentous events. He despises active resistance to any change in his belief.

However, experts say racial prejudice could easily become a thing of the past. Racial attitudes can change very quickly. In 1942, most Americans agreed, "There should be separate sections for Negroes on streetcars and buses," reported H. H. Hyman & P. B. Sheatsley in their 1954 study. Has this changed?

After 45 years Dr. T. F. Pettigrew, a research professor of social psychology at the UCSC affirmed in 1987: "Many [people] have confessed to me … that even though in their minds they no longer feel prejudice towards Black people, they still feel squeamish when they shake hands with a black. These feelings are left over from what they learned in their families as children."

Subtle

'*Subtle prejudice*' is a relatively contemporary concept identified by social scientists as 'modern racism' or 'cultural racism.' Modern prejudice is a euphemism for what is familiar, favorable, and comfortable, wrote Dr. J. F. Dovidio, et al. and Dr. V. M. Esses, et al. in their studies.

"In India, people who accept the caste system will typically allow someone from a lower caste into their homes but would not consider marrying such a person," wrote Dr. N. Sharma in 1981.

Or take this national survey of Americans reported by Dr. W. A. Henry in 1994, where 75 percent said they would "shop at a store owned by a homosexual", but only 39 percent would "see a homosexual doctor." This is only two-and-a-half decades ago when The American Supreme Court declared same-sex marriage as legal in all 50 US states in 2015.

Racism is more than skin deep. My meliorism-kibitzer friend quips, "Racism is like dust in the air. It is always present but often never seen. However, with a flashlight or sunbeam positioned in the proper angle, in the right place, at the right time, the phenomenon of dust appears."

Zeitgeist, anyone?

To bribe or not to bribe for college admission

By Dr. Aggie Carson-Arenas
Columnist, Inquirer, US Bureau, April 4, 2019

Richie owns several apartment buildings and other businesses in Pampanga and is legally married to a woman. The couple is well-off, albeit in a not *filthy lucre* fashion.

The wife was pregnant with their first child. "*Hinding Hindi tatapak sa lupa ang mega anak ko,*" (Never will my children trend on the soil/ground) in a similar tone my father said to my mom before we were born, she claimed. I often overheard her tell her friends when I and my medical doctor brother were growing up.

"*Mag-aaral sila sa* La Salle, Letran, Ateneo, St. Scholastica, Assumption (My children will be well provided, will study in elite school)," haughtily declared Richie to my mom, during a business-social visit where I tagged along as her driver.

After many decades, this scene comes to mind upon reading the recent big news about the college admission scandal, which could possibly be the biggest bribery scandal in American college history.

Almost 50 individuals, including more than 30 parents, have been indicted by the U.S. Attorney for allegedly conspiring to get underperforming students into some of the country's most prestigious colleges and universities.

Parents, including celebrities, used bribes ranging from a few thousand dollars up to $6 million, or a whopping 312 million pesos (1:52 rate of exchange). Is it worth it?

Empirical observations indicate that college admissions (frankly, any human *struggle* promoting "equality") should be based on merit and challenging work, intelligence, diligence, and hard-earned credentials rather than wealth or lineage.

However, my jack-of-all-trades-analyst kibitzer friend quips, "Money is the root of evil, education the root of development." Would coalescing evil and development hurt?

Going to any college has two main purposes: enhance prospects for *career success*, which likely equates to monetary and material wealth; and acquiring *social status*, prestige, fame, power and glory.

One would think that the rich and famous would care less than the rest of us about securing a spot for their children in elite colleges. After all, their kids are likely to be financially secure no matter where, or if, they go to college.

It seems the primary purpose of those indicted in this case was for "social status"? This is akin to the *psychic secretion* we learn in the Pavlov's dog experiment in general psychology. Mere ideation or association can trigger observable physiological reaction, which I can prove below.

Imagine a slice of greenish-raw mango from Bataan... top this with a teaspoon of *bagoong* (a Filipino paste-condiment made from fermented anchovies or small fish), savor the flavor... now... take a bite. This explains psychic secretion: salivation by ideation. (Caveat: this might be observable among Filipinos only).

Is this what a few wants for most of us to feel because they are Ivy Leaguers?

Reality

College is college — some schools have more to offer than others; but in our life, we are going to meet plenty of useless dingbats who went to the most distinguished colleges in the country. We will also encounter wizards who barely went to school at all, wrote Jason Gay in the *Wall Street Journal*.

The reality, however, is wealthy and privileged people have always had an educational leg up, like Richie. With money comes access to the best neighborhoods and the best schools with the smallest class sizes and richest resources and best teachers.

With money comes better tutoring, test prep or review, enrichment and after-school activities, all of which provide avenues into top colleges, writes D. Braff of *The Washington Post*.

Somehow, college is not for everyone. Bonnie Goldstein writes in the *USA Today* that it cost him $50,000 to figure out that his son did not want to go to college. His son got a half dozen acceptance letters who even let him choose which school was best for him!

When the son got there, he threw up during the orientation and spent his whole first semester never attending a class. Goldstein later admitted: To succeed in college, even kids with limitless advantages *must want* to be there.

High school years are supposed to be a developmental and exploratory period for career planning. A student is expected to seek knowledge, get some insight on how to reach firm scholastic commitments.

Worth

When parents are willing to bribe someone to admit their children to Ivy League schools, they are risking their reputations and wealth because they would be committing an illegal act. Is it worth it?

We are reminded that, instead of pointing fingers at the parents or celebrities who leveraged their wealth to give their children a big, albeit very unfair, boost, who is to say that some of us would not do the same if we had the money and the power to ensure our child's education? inquired D. Braff of the *Washington Post*.

If you are (really) rich, you are going to have a leg up; you will be able to have the financial wherewithal to affect the outcome in ways that families with lesser resources would not, stated Audie Cornish on an *NPR* talk. This is the way it is always been, particularly at elite schools.

Elite schools do not have two lines, one for ordinary applicants and one for the wealthy. They will say that you get in based on your test scores, grades and your recommendations and so on.

The overall percentage of alumni who donate to universities is dwindling. So, schools are very dependent on big donors, the kind who give enough money to secure an admission.

Jared Kushner, President Donald Trump's son-in-law and senior adviser is among those whose college admission seems to have been helped by contributions by a wealthy parent, hints a 2006 book "*The Price of Admission: How America's Ruling Class Buys Its Way into Elite Colleges — and Who Gets Left Outside the Gates.*"

Meritocracy

Meritocracy is when one's "power" stems from one's own knowledge, abilities, aptitudes, interests, talents, efforts and achievement, rather than on race, gender, age or wealth or behest opportunity. But meritocracy is an illusion, bluntly stated Jason Gay of *The Wall Street Journal*; because long before an application shows up at a school, the system is legitimately stacked in favor of the wealthy. Children who are not from privileged backgrounds are at a steep disadvantage, simply because they cannot afford the add-on accoutrements.

How many parents are (actually) buying their children's admission into college? Again, according to Jason Gay, there is a hallowed tradition of admitting the mediocre spawn of the moneyed. On many campuses, you will find inspired buildings bankrolled by the families of uninspired brains.

There is the rub. If you look closer inside some privately own academic institutions, you may be greeted by wall-to-wall plaques emblazoned with names of philanthropic donors, from the richest to the filthy rich and famous or elected politicians. Many represented names are likely bestowed with academic awards; some are elected as trustee or board members or conferred with honorary degree of sort. The façade it represents of course is legal, so we are told.

Imee's case

If you attended school at the University of the Philippines (UP) main campus, you may have heard through the grapevine, "*Anak na nang presidente, na kick-out pa...*" (In spite of being a president's daughter, she was "kicked-out."

The president's daughter was not actually "kicked-out," UP students protested her graduation, demanded to show proof of her academic records. Records indicated that she lacked 35 units and appeared have never had the proper qualification to enter school.

Records also show that her name does not appear on the approved graduates list, nor was she among the candidates endorsed by the graduation committee at the time, writes Ricardo Manapat in the book, *Some are Smarter than Others*, in 1991.

Eat your heart out, Ivy League.

Teens' brains, technology amid the pandemic

By Dr. Aggie Carson-Arenas
Columnist, Inquirer, US Bureau, November 26, 2020

"The razor-toothed piranhas of the genera *Serrasalmus* and *Pygocentrus* are the most ferocious freshwater fish in the world. In reality they seldom attack a human." This was the phrase texted in 18.19 seconds by Marcel Fernandes, a 16-year-old physics student at a university in Florianópolis, Brazil, the speediest texter in the world.

Technically, in psychological terms, Fernandes demonstrated to the world his *psychomotor threshold*. Psychomotor is a clinical term relating to 'motor action' (finger texting behavior) directly proceeding from 'mental activity' (cognition). Both are brain driven. The question is what makes Fernandes the world's cogent psychomotor dandy.

How is technology affecting the collective brain, behavior and emotion of millions of adolescents currently locked down during this Covid saeculum?

Neo-polymath

The 16-year-old Brazilian physics student apparently has a lot of cognitive gray matter in his young brain. This is likely fused with tons of *engrams*— the theorized "physical" cognitive information in the brain, which Fernandes seems to manifest through speed-texting.

In the realm of psychology, cognition generally equates with *intelligence*, which encompasses cognition or the process by which Fernandes might be taking in and integrating knowledge we know as "intelligence."

"The past half-century has seen a dramatic increase in the amount of technology available to and used by children — a fact that has clearly shaped the way children learn, develop, and behave," according to Dr. D. Bavelier, a French cognitive neuroscientist at the University of Geneva.

Empirical studies also show that technological gizmos have turned millions of teenagers or adolescents into some type of intellectual savvies. Their cognitive potential is probably or at least appearing at par with rare polymaths of the pre-computer era. Is technology affecting Fernandes' brain or is his brain simply adapting to technology?

Studies

Three decades ago, the late Dr. D. F. Klein then director of Research at New York Psychiatric Institute observed that animals exposed to an "enriched environment have larger cerebral cortices, more glial cells, bigger neurons, more active neurotransmitters, and larger blood supplies to the brain than animals in control group."

Dr. Klein's later suggested, "Kids raised in a smart, responsive environment, which is complex and stimulating, may develop a different set of skills. If kids can call on the environment to do things for them, they become less dependent on parents at a younger age."

The multi-instant tasking digital gadgets of kids today seem to fit this benchmark, quips my computer savvy kibitzer friend. Today's tech-gizmos are portable, accessible 24/7, instantaneous, omnipresent, and seem omnipotent.

Moreover, again according to Dr. Klein, "These kids may gain a sense of competence; they can afford to be inquisitive, exploratory, imaginative, and to adopt a problem-solving approach to life. All of which may *promote changes* in the brain itself."

"It is not impossible that an intelligent environment (technology) could lead us to develop new synapses and a larger cortex. A smarter environment might make smarter people." We are reminded that many current studies are anchored on this theory proposed more than 30 years ago by Dr. Klein.

"At this point, all we can do is guess," declared Dr. Klein in the 1990s. Is the guessing game he brought forth over? Unfortunately interrupted by the Covid-19? inquiringly quipped my cynical kibitzer friend.

Exposure

"Daily exposure to high technology stimulates brain cell alteration and neurotransmitter release, gradually strengthening new neural pathways in our brains (while weakening old ones)," according to Drs. G. Small and G. Vorgan, in the *Scientific American Mind* recently downloaded in 2019.

Drs. G. Small and G. Vorgan's, earlier study suggested that people working on the Internet for several hours without a break report making frequent errors in their work. Upon signing off, many notice feeling fatigued, irritable and distracted, or simply spaced out, experiencing "digital fog."

This *digital fog* state was coined by Dr. G. Small to mean "techno-brain burnout." This stressful state threatens to become an epidemic and is probably already affecting many more teenagers due to lockdowns caused by Covid-19.

Empirical studies also suggest that the brain's neural circuitry responds constantly to whatever sensory activities we are involved. This includes time we spend surfing the Internet, iChatting, e-mailing, and e-shopping. Apparently, these online processes continually and digitally stimulate the brain.

Dr. P. Moore wrote in the *Inferential Focus Briefing* article as early as 1997 that "teenagers use different parts of their brain and think in different ways than adults when at the computer." Does reading tons of books have the same "effect" on the brain, inquired my bookworm kibitzer friend.

Parker-Pope, in her article, *Surfing the Internet Boosts Aging Brains*, clarified, "Compared with reading, the Internet's wealth of choices requires that individuals make decisions about what to click on, which is an activity that engages important cognitive circuits in the brain." "Real time" is really "real" online, unlike reading a book that depends on mere ideation and imagination, quipped my cynical kibitzer friend.

Consequence

A teenager can run several instant messages simultaneously demonstrate how certain younger brains can function with speed, like Fernandes. These younger brains obviously acquired basic training from the rapid-fire digital gizmos they have 24/7 access into; gaining astonishing velocities influencing how they think (cognition).

"Besides influencing how we think, digital technology is altering how we *feel*, how we *behave*," again according to Drs. G, Small and G. Vorgan. 'Feeling' and 'behavior' are linked to emotion. Millions if not all of teenagers rely on digital connectivity for entertainment to communications and to almost everything.

Drs. G. Small and G. Vorgan's study also suggested that "As the brain evolves and shifts its focus toward new technological skills, it drifts away from fundamental social skills, such as reading facial expressions during conversation or grasping the emotional context of a subtle gesture."

As early as 2002, a Stanford University study revealed that "for every hour we spend on our computers, traditional face-to-face interaction time with other people drops by nearly 30 minutes." An hour a day of online searches changes the way the brain processes information.

A constant barrage of e-contacts is stimulating, sharpening certain cognitive skills, yet draining at the same time. This creates significant disequilibrium between cognitive and emotional development among teenagers revealed akin studies.

The rub, according to Dr. A. Damasio, a world-renowned neuroscientist and prolific writer, "The risk of emotional neutrality becomes greater and greater as the speed of cognition increases. There will be more and more people who will have to rely on the cognitive system entirely, without using their emotional memory, to decide what is good and what is evil."

Similarly, another UCLA study suggested, "While the brains of today's *digital natives* (referring to tech-sodden teenagers) are wiring up for rapid-fire cyber searches, however, the neural circuits that control the more traditional learning methods are neglected and gradually diminished."

This simply means, "The pathways for human interaction and communication weaken as customary one-on-one people skills atrophy." Is this made more complicated due to the home lockdown of teenagers?

Finally

Evolutionary theorists tell us that the human brain evolves only after so many millions of years due to lack of "evolutionary technology" available at that (particular) era. Today, new technological breakthrough occurs constantly or sometimes in just a few months.

The Covid vaccine seems "almost" ready only after a few months, which my reticent-kibitzer friend quipped "is tacitly an AI assisted process, otherwise just to complete the rigorous laboratory trials would take many, many years."

Computer memory started with a few kilobytes. Today gigabytes are getting cheaper, common and rapidly outstripped by terabytes then petabytes (PB). Currently, we have the Exabyte (EB) where there are 1,024 PB in an Exabyte (EB). Only Google has an estimated 15 EB data held.

Nerveless, the result of "too much information" is not a danger that our cognitive machinery will short out. We can in fact process all that data, our brain will not explode or implode due to data explosions, quipped my mentalist kibitzer friend .

The *danger* and perhaps more, comes from the emotional system's shorting out, so we are told.

The computer is the mother of contemporary technology, wrote my alter-ego-kibitzer friend. It is subtly molding our behavior for the future. Its impact is now patent in the *bioelectrochemical* of the brain as contemporary studies unfold the ubiquitous overwhelming effect of technological breakthrough to our cognition and emotion.

However, the danger of our high-speed society — caused by high-speed technology — in coming generations is not that teenagers will be overloaded by information; it is that they will become brilliant on all the cognitive or intelligence tests but devoid of emotion that could be ethically rudderless, so we are told again.

An early *psychosocial* intervention among lockdown home kids is but one solution to mitigate a new generation of adult-enablers with too much intelligence but with impaired emotional quotients. Will a future physicist-Fernandes refute the context of this piece?

A kid left out without early, timely and appropriate intervention? Your guess is as good as anybody's.

Did 'Wonder Woman' inspire the lie detector?
by Dr. Aggie Carson-Arenas
Columnist, Inquirer, US Bureau, September 19, 2018

Wonder Woman and Steve Trevor were depicted using systolic blood pressure measurements at times to identify liars, spies, and signs of deceptions in the comic strips "Wonder Woman," *Sensation Comics*#3, Wonder Woman#4 circa 1942. Many believe these scenes inspired the "lie detector."

The comic series was created by William Marston, to whom the polygraph "invention" was erroneously attributed. It was John Lorson, a policeman who invented the modern polygraph; the first American police officer bestowed an academic doctorate for the use of polygraph in criminal investigations. Leonarde Keeler is the co-inventor of Larson's "cardio-pneumo-psychogram."

The creator of Wonder Woman was a forensic and legal psychologist who first utilized the "tool" in courtrooms during his practice, which could have caused the confusion. The *Committee to Review the Scientific Evidence on the Polygraph* in 2003 recognized Marston for "measuring physiological reactions" in attempting to evaluate honesty in criminal proceedings.

Did Marston ever believe in the efficacy or veracity of the results of this invention that was partially attributed to him?

Measure

Polygraph does not detect lies. It measures human physiological reactions associated with bodily equilibrium. Any disruption in the biopsychological due to stress or any bodily *disequilibrium* leads to, or is manifested in, physiological reactions collectively known as "human emotions." A polygraph likely really is an "emotion detector."

A polygraph simply detects then "translates" emotional reactions into quantifiable lines-in-graph based on one's physiological reactions. This may be like how as an observable indicator of emotion; Pinocchio shows the telltale sign of an extending nose whenever *someone* somewhere lies.

A polygraph is basically a physiological recorder. It assesses three indicators of autonomic arousal: heart rate/blood pressure; respiration; skin conductivity or sweating. Respiration rate and depth are measured by *pneumographs* wrapped around a respondent's chest. Cardiovascular activity is monitored by a *blood pressure cuff.* Skin conductivity or sweating is gauged through *electrodes* attached to a respondent's fingertips.

Polygraph records physiological changes during emotion, i.e., during an "interrogation." Its application is based on the theory that a suspect — guilty of a crime — will be more emotionally aroused by questions relevant to the "crime."

The often seemingly subtle emotions manifested by a suspect during "interrogation" are objectively "recorded" by the polygraph making a graph of each of the bodily changes as they occur during emotion.

The rub is, as a study by David Lykken suggested in 1981, there is no unique "lie response" that everyone gives when *not* telling the truth. The machine only records general emotional arousal — it cannot tell the difference between lying and fear, anxiety, or excitement.

Infallible

Many people believe that a polygraph is an infallible *scientific* instrument and place confidence in its results. The instrument is based on a cogent psychological principle: humans are likely to become physiologically "stirred up" when they feel so threatened by a question that they answer it untruthfully.

However, many studies suggest that a perfectly innocent person may react emotionally to a critical inquiry — and thus appear to be lying when actually telling the truth, due to many influencing variables such as individual constitutions, cultural influences, potential examiner's biased impressions, "training" as the KGB had learned long ago, or mental state.

In forensic psychology for instance, a diagnosed pathological liar or sociopath can feel no anxiety or guilt about anything and thus tell outrageous untruths without showing the slightest emotional ripple, according to American psychologists Kleinnuntz and Szucko in 1984.

A pioneering study by psychologist Lykken showed that polygraph tests could be "fooled" or countered by secretly invoking alternative sensations at the same time, which can confuse the polygraph by merely biting the tongue or constricting the anal sphincter. The use of any ideational altering-arousal strategies could be as effective.

Law

In 1983, the Congressional Office of Technology Assessment (U.S. Congress, 1983, P: 4) warned that, the available research evidence does not establish the scientific validity of the polygraph test for personnel security screening.

Three years after, the American Psychological Association (APA) issued a formal statement in part, "…has great reservations about the use of polygraph tests to detect deception." The polygraph test has been deemed too inaccurate for most state courts, and polygraph evidence is not admissible in half the states according to Lykken in 1985.

The U.S. Congress in 1988 passed a law *strictly limiting* the use of lie detector tests for job applicants and employees of private businesses. However, it allowed wide "application" mostly among business sectors. Experts (likely lawyers) forewarn that any employee could be given a lie detector test; the best advice is to remain calm *then* actively challenge the outcome of the instrument that erroneously questions your honesty (!).

Some experts nevertheless aver that the polygraph functions more appropriately as a tool in criminal investigation. Police sometimes use the polygraph to induce confessions by criminals who are scared into thinking that their lies are transparent. Does this mean finding the "right sucker" to "psych"? inquired my kibitzer friend.

Moreover, courts, including the United States Supreme Court (cf. U.S. v. Scheffer, 1998), have repeatedly rejected the use of polygraph evidence because of its inherent unreliability; despite it still wide usage.

Witchcraft

Studies suggest that polygraph "testing" is a thriving American industry. However, how much personal, legal, and administrative decisions were unfairly influenced or distorted by its results? This is good evidence of psychology misapplied; how psychological principles can be warped when its findings are used unsystematically.

Undoubtedly the validity of polygraph testing remains shrouded in controversies. An underlying problem is *theoretical*: There is no evidence that any pattern of physiological reactions is unique to deception. An honest person may be nervous when answering truthfully and a dishonest person may be non-anxious, according to Dr. Saxe of Brandeis University.

Drs. Leonard Sexe with colleague Gershon BenShahar, also revealed that there are few good studies that validate the ability of polygraph procedures to detect deception. However, both affirmed, it may, in fact, be impossible to conduct a proper validity study. In real-world situations, it's exceedingly difficult to know what the truth is.

Did the *Wonder Woman* creator, who popularized the "lie detector," never waver in believing its efficacy or veracious results? Record shows that Marston appeared as the lie detection expert in a landmark court; the case that led an appellate court to rule and set the enduring legal standard that his own lie detection method should not be admissible in court.

Moreover, polygraph tests are sometimes used in seeking to convince others of their innocence. Have you heard about the senator who was accused of committing a crime whereby his lawyer unabashedly recommended he take a private lie-detector test? If he *passed*, they should announce pronto the results in a press conference.

"The 'lie detector' is modern 'witchcraft,'" retorts my kibitzer friend.

Only Wonder Woman can refute.

Toxic words are hazardous to your health

By Dr. Aggie Carson-Arenas
Columnist, Inquirer, US Bureau, November 19, 2018

Auntie M was diagnosed with cancer. Dr. S. presented the diagnosis to her son who was then attending med school. The verdict: *"Siguro, anim hanggang walong buwan* (Maybe, six to eight months). Imagine the anxiety caused by these mere five words to a whole clan.

The son completed med school, was taking his residency in internal medicine when in a twist of fate happened to meet Dr. S., who greeted him: *"Kumusta na ang Nanay mo… buhay pa?"* "(How is your Mom, still alive?). *"Muntik ko nang bigwasan* (Almost gave him a smack on the face) said the son-G about this incident.

The apparently disconcerting, emotionally devoid "words" uttered by Dr. S. could have derailed G's medical career. The good news is Auntie Melly is well, still alive after several decades to see her two grandchildren grow up. Dr. G is a medical doctor in North Carolina; he's my cousin, so I know.

Elusive

"Words matter," was the favorite catchword during the last mid-term elections. A truism studied almost by every discipline, from anthropology to zoology. The elusive question is *why*?

Many practitioners of the healing art estimate that 50% to 80% of patients who consult medical doctors basically suffer from *functional disorders*. Disorders of this kind are thought to originate from the mind; often no lucid or precise physiological basis could be established.

Mental experiences from insinuation, claim, rhetoric, or even diagnoses — real or truth, erroneous, fake, or mere ideation — can interrupt or disrupt the normal systemic functions of the body known as *homeostasis*; something like an "internal thermostat." Homeostasis includes the endocrinal and immunological balance, blood supply and pressure, respiration pattern, and digestive processes, among others.

Studies show that in conjunction with other allied body systems such as the *autonomic nervous system* (ANS), psychological disequilibrium, homeostasis "disturbed" for whatever reasons, such as stress, could affect internal body activities to react or malfunction. Subsequently, this could lead to some form of seemingly pure-physical ailments such as peptic ulcer, asthma, and migraine (among trillion others).

Iatrogenic

Empirical studies reveal that daily bombardment of "words" (*aka*, news, blogs, rhetoric) by contemporary multimedia trolls and bots can take a toll or present stress on anyone.

J. and F. Saunders as early as the '70s identified responses of body to stress. Take peptic ulcer. This ailment from the excessive secretion of gastric acid that irritates, inflames, and ultimately breaks the stomach wall is caused by stress resulting from mental experiences.

In other words, an "unquantifiable mental experience" like stress could become a physiological ailment. Recent studies undoubtedly reveal that a certain dormant bacterium, *Helicobacter pylori*, in the stomach could be the culprit causing ulcer; nevertheless, the *mystique remains*: What triggers the activation of these bacteria to cause harm?

Moreover, *iatrogenic*, an obscure or less-quoted term, is defined by the American Psychological Association's Dictionary of Psychology as denoting or relating to a disease or pathological condition that is inadvertently caused by treatment.

'Iatrogenic' is probably the most despised term in medicine, also meaning an induced and/or aggravated medical condition due to a doctor's diagnosis/misdiagnosis. Diagnoses are words presented by an *assumed expert* (doctor) to an *assumed subordinate* (patient).

Suggestibility

All human beings have an innate suggestibility, or proneness to suggestion. Suggestion simply means presenting an idea to another often to elicit motor, mental, or similar responses. People are deemed suggestible if they accept and act on suggestions by others.

A person experiencing intense emotions, according to Myers, author of various psychology books, tends to be more receptive to ideas, thus is more suggestible. Also, psychologists have identified that individual levels of self-esteem, assertiveness, circumstance, among others, can make some people more suggestible than others, as depicted in the following vignette.

Kenneth Arnold, while piloting his private plane near Mount Rainier on June 24, 1947, spotted nine glittering objects in the sky. Thinking these were foreign guided missiles (barely two years after WWII), he attempted reporting the incident to the FBI.

Unfortunately, the FBI office was closed; he instead went to his local newspaper reporting, "Crescent-shaped objects that moved like a saucer would if you skipped it across the water." This was quoted by the

Associated Press, then reported in more than 150 newspapers as the sighting of "saucers." The term "flying saucers" was born, triggering a worldwide wave of "flying saucer sightings" during the rest of the summer of 1949.

The spread of such "affecting" information is common today due to the ubiquitous Internet. "Have you heard about the *deepfake* technology that will roil what remains of our consciousness?" inquired my tech-savvy kibitzer friend.

Moreover, who would believe that a tooth extraction could be done without an iota of anesthesia! Have you heard of *hypnodontia*, where hypnotic suggestion can zap excruciating pain during a dental procedure?

Why do words matter? Sigmund Freud explained this 150 years ago.

The power of adolescents

By Dr. Aggie Carson-Arenas
Columnist, Inquirer, US Bureau, March 6, 2018

"There is hope in the next generation... I'm optimistic about our kids, always," stated former first lady Michelle Obama as she offered praises for the Florida students who were shooting survivors and have been speaking out for gun control.

These students are "kids" in their adolescence. Does Mrs. Obama's praise for the adolescent shooting survivors sound familiar?

More than a century ago, an 18-year-old adolescent wrote and dedicated a poem to the youth of his time, winning him first prize in a poetry contest. This adolescent was Pepe, later Dr. Jose Rizal who became the National Hero of the Philippine. Rizal was executed by the Spanish colonial authorities at the age of 35.

"*Ang kabataan ang pag-asa ng bayan* (The youth is the hope of the fatherland)" is the famous quote from Pepe's poem. The poem was entitled, "A La Juventud Filipina (To the Filipino Youth)."

The context of this quote presumably is still relevant today, from Mrs. Obama's perspective.

This quote has been rephrased, interpreted and contextualized in so many ways, perhaps one of the latest presented by the World Health Organization (WHO) in 2015: Adolescents are the greatest resource for a society to thrive.

Power of many

Studies show that there are about 1.2 billion individuals aged 10 to

19; or one in six (1:6) of the world's population who are categorized as adolescents. The Florida students shooting survivors are part of this 1.2 billion.\

In the Philippine alone, there were 18 million aged 15-24, comprising 19.6 or almost 20 percent of the total population in 2010. This is projected to expand further in the near future, reaching a historical peak of 22.2 million in 2040, according to the Philippine Statistics Authority (PSA).

These numbers suggest that as a collective unit, adolescence have the capacity to influence many sectors of society. Adolescents could be the great lifestyle-disrupters ever; dubbed the Post-Millennials, Gen-Z, or simply iGen. Their power extends from birth control compliance and the patronage of Uber,® to mastery of social media technology, and "child activism" or #NeverAgain advocacy.

Greatest resource

WHO organization has been encouraging every nation to invest in adolescence for a three-pronged benefit: healthy adolescents are benefited now; they become healthy adults in the future; healthy adults lead to a thriving next generation.

Healthy adolescents now – When adolescents of today are provided the right support and opportunity, taught positive habits, equipped with constructive forms of risk-taking; prevented from and provided with treatment for such problems as substance use, mental disorders, and injuries, they are immediately benefited.

Healthy adults in the future – When adolescents are supported and inculcated with healthy behaviors during adolescence such as proper diet, physical activity, and — if sexually active — safe-sex practices, reduced use of alcohol or illicit drugs, it is a good start in setting a pattern of healthy lifestyles, thereby reducing disability and premature mortality later in adulthood.

Healthy future generations – When adolescents accumulate healthy practices; good physical and mental hygiene and recognize prevention of risk factors during adulthood; they tend to achieve a balanced wellbeing. Well-balanced adults help protect the health (body and mind) of the next generations' offspring.

Moreover, when adolescents are healthy, they bring economic benefits to society. They become more productive; their health costs are reduced thus enhancing social capital. A social capital that is harmonious, functioning, and mutually supportive, it is a more powerful asset than any advocacy.

The healthier adolescents are in body and mind, the more productive they become, and the happier they will be enjoying the best quality of life.

Gautama Buddha a great philosopher in 563 BCE, reminded us that to keep the body in good health is a duty; otherwise, we shall not be able to keep our mind strong and clear.

Reminder

The Florida shooting survivors are in their adolescence; many are often already in a precarious transition between childhood and adulthood due to the significant changes in their physical, cognitive, moral, and social development.

Many are likely experiencing the "stress and storm" of adolescence. Would the #NeverAgain movement burden them somehow?

Maybe not. Studies remind us that resiliency is also a great, salient reserve during adolescence... This could be a positive component of their learning process.

"They are smart, they are passionate, and they do have the right values. They know inequity. They know wrong when they see it. There is hope in that next generation. They're tired of watching us do the same old thing and expect different results," again, according to Mrs. Obama.

Moreover, Dr. Flavia Bustreo, WHO Assistant Director-General in 2016 stated, "Adolescents have been entirely absent from national health plans for decades," which obviously must include mental health plans as well.

A relatively small investment focused on adolescents now will not only result in healthy and empowered adults who thrive and contribute positively to their communities, but it will also result in healthier future generations, yielding enormous returns.

So, would #NeverAgain's efforts to protect school children from gun violence win this time around? Would adult lawmakers decide to invest in the youth for the benefit of all?

Your guess is as good as mine.

Mental stresses may impact immigrant kids separated from parents

By Dr. Aggie Carson-Arenas
Columnist, Inquirer, US Bureau, June 6, 2018

One thousand four hundred seventy-five (1,475) out of the 7,635 unaccompanied immigrant children were reported unaccounted (lost track of) during the last quarter of 2017. These children were placed in an Office of the Refugee Resettlement (ORR) shelter by the federal government.

The majority of such children are sent to live with sponsors who have close ties with them — typically a parent or close relative. Some, however, end up living with "other-than-close relatives," or non-relatives, according to Steven Wagner, a top official with the Department of Health and Human Services (HHS).

The children are *not lost*, according to the HHS Deputy Secretary Eric Horgan, just *can't be reached.*

Context

Deputy Horgan is likely speaking in a bureaucratic sense, seemingly negating the consequences of the adverse effect of parental separation on children.

There is such thing as "separation anxiety," the normal alarm or fear experienced by a young child separated from the persons or caregivers to whom a child is attached, particularly parents. Separation anxiety is most active among children between 6 and 10 months old. However, separation from loved ones in later years may elicit similar anxiety.

Separation anxiety disorder according to the American Psychiatric Association's (APA) bible-of-mental-disorder or the *Diagnostic*

Statistical Manual (DSM-IV-TR) is characterized by developmentally inappropriate, persistent, and excessive anxiety about separation from the home or from major attachment figures.

Some of the pronounced symptoms may be fear of being alone or going to sleep without the major attachment figures, separation-related nightmares, and repeated complaints of physical symptoms (e.g., vomiting, nausea, headaches, or stomachaches). These symptoms cause clinically significant distress or impairment in functioning.

Apparently, these "separated" children are already entangled in ponderous strife; moreover, they are also still developing beings who are in a unique, often precarious, relatively short phase of human development within a delicately prescribed timeframe.

Any disruption (bureaucratic, physical or mental) during this phase, like imposed or "lawful" familial separations would have adverse consequences manifested later in life. No one can reverse time to rectify the effect(s) of a prior-disrupted phase on their bio-psycho-socio development, unless through a sound psychosocial rehabilitative intervention or therapy.

Bureaucratic to neural to DNA

Physicians Vincent Felitti and Robert Anda coined *Adverse Childhood Experiences (ACEs)* to encompass the chronic, unpredictable, and stress-inducing events that some children face. Doctors Felitti and Anday studied the histories of 17,000 youths in 1995.

The results were shocking: Nearly two thirds of children had encountered one or more ACEs, such as growing up with a depressed or alcoholic parent; losing a parent to divorce or other causes (e.g., separation); or enduring chronic humiliation, emotional neglect, or sexual or physical abuse. These forms of emotional trauma went beyond the typical, everyday challenges of growing up, according to Felitti and Anda.

Other studies reveal that experiencing chronic, unpredictable toxic stress during childhood predisposes children to a constellation of chronic conditions in adulthood. These adversities are now recognized as more far more prevalent than researchers had imagined, according to Dr. Janice Kiecolt-Glaser, College of Medicine, Ohio State University.

How do childhood chronic adversities or stresses get under the skin way to affect risk of later physical and behavioral ailments in adolescence to adulthood?

Today, according to Donna Jackson Nakazawa, author of *The Autoimmune Epidemic* and the *Last Best Cure*, in labs across the country, neuroscientists are peering into the once inscrutable brain-body connection, and breaking down, on a biochemical level, exactly how the stress we face as children catches up with us when we are adults, altering our bodies, our cells, and even our DNA.

We are forewarned that contemporary scientific findings can be a little overwhelming to contemplate.

Studies, for instance, show that when the developing brain is chronically stressed, it releases a hormone that actually shrinks the size of the hippocampus, an area of the brain responsible of processing emotion and memory and managing stress (per reveal by recent magnetic resonance imaging [MRI] results).

MRI studies also suggest that the higher an individual's ACE Score, the less gray matter an individual has in other key areas of the brain, including the prefrontal cortex, which is related to decision-making and self-regulatory skills, and the amygdala or fear-processing center.

Dr. Ryan Herringa, neuropsychiatrist and assistant professor of child and adolescent psychiatry at the University of Wisconsin, reports that children whose brains have been changed by their *Adverse Childhood Experiences* are more likely to become adults who find themselves over-reacting to even minor stressors.

The deduction by these studies suggest that children who come into adolescence with a history of adversity and lack the presence of a consistent, loving adult to help them through it may become more likely to develop mood disorders or have poor executive functioning and decision-making skills.

Thus, their cognitive and moral reasoning capabilities are simply riled and compromised.

Any "bureaucrat" need not have the brain of a rocket scientist to recognize that this could be one possible, potential and lethal root of contemporary school violence? This is basic psychology, an understanding of which some creators-of-man's-law seem to lack.

Moreover, we are reminded that 29% of the *Deferred Action for Childhood Arrivals* or DACA recipients are in ages 16 to 20 and 365,000 are high school students across the United States.

Quo Vadis, Mr. Bureaucrat?

To be or not to be LGBTQ

By Dr. Aggie Carson-Arenas
Columnist, Inquirer, US Bureau, July 1, 2019

"I do not gender my child," expressed a biological mother Kori Doty, a non-binary transgender Canadian.

"It is up to Searyl to decide how they identify, when they are old enough to develop their own gender identity" (Kori prefers the pronouns "they/their.") "I am not going to foreclose their choices based on an arbitrary assignment of gender at birth based on an inspection of their genitals."

Searyl Atli Doty is said to be the world's first person issued a genderless government ID card from the British Columbia Medical Services Plan almost three years ago. Kori is affiliated with the *Gender-Free I. D. Coalition,* a group advocating for genderless government documents in Canada.

According to an oft-quoted study by John Gonsiorek, we cannot willfully choose or easily change our sexual orientation. Our sexual orientation is like handedness that endures; we could be right-handed, left-handed or ambidextrous that is a deep part of our personal identity.

Being gay is not a personal choice because an individual is simply devoid of choice in the matter. How many are perturbed, struggling, wrestling with his/her sexual orientation? Is it (really) as "a kind of war?" as one presidential candidate professes?

Cause

Homosexuality is often linked with issues in a child's psychological relationships with parents: a domineering mother and a weak, ineffectual father; or a possessive, "seductive" mother and a hostile father; or molestation by an adult homosexual.

But is homosexuality encoded in biology, in our genes?

Current findings tend to discredit myths about parental behaviors that make children homosexual, as well as the claim that homosexuality is merely a preference. While learning contributes to one's sexual orientation, it appears that nature strongly prepares people to be either homosexual or heterosexual, stated in 2012 by Dr. Simon LeVay, a neuroscientist studying the biological and genetic roots of homosexuality.

Dr. LeVay stated during a radio interview on the WBUR talk show several years ago that, "half the reason why an individual is gay or straight is genetic -- what the other half is we don't know." There's the rub.

Studies also refuted these widely held ideas about the causes of homosexuality. A comprehensive survey in search of the psychological causes of homosexuality, the Kinsey Institute queried nearly 1,000 homosexuals and 500 heterosexuals.

The result: Apart from homosexual feelings and a somewhat greater attitude of non-conformity, the backgrounds of homosexuals and heterosexuals are the same.

However, despite of findings suggesting that homosexuality is part of the normal range of variations in sexual orientation, a homosexual individual who has nothing inherently wrong with him/her still encounters hostility.

Homosexuals tend to experience rejection by family members, employment discrimination and the unfavorable sentiments based on stereotypes of gay and lesbian individuals, or simple ignorance or rejection of scientific results, or religious zealotry.

Conversion therapy

Mayor of South Bench, Indiana Pete Buttigieg is the second openly gay presidential candidate in history. He criticized Vice President Mike Pence, a conservative Christian known for signing the Indiana Religious Freedom Restoration Act in 2015, which allows businesses to deny service to LGBTQ persons on religious grounds and who also supported the funding of *conversion therapy* in 2000.

Conversion therapy is a kind of "treatment," involving counseling and psychotherapy, which attempts to eliminate an individual's sexual desires for members of his/her own sex. This is basically a clinical attempt to change an individual's sexual orientation.

Studies reveal that conversion therapy is among the so-called "reparative therapies" for "fixing" something that is not a mental illness and, therefore, does not require therapy. This therapeutic technique has been banned in several states in America since 2013. There is no scientific evidence that conversion therapy works, and it can potentially harm the client according to the American Psychological Association (APA) President Barry S. Anton, PhD in 2015.

Sameness

Studies consistently show that the capacity for emotional adjustment, whether an individual is a heterosexual or homosexual, appears similar. Sexual orientation has no bearing on his/her ability to function in society, work constructively, maintain mental health, and care for children, or form caring relationships. Therefore, homosexuality was delisted as a sexual disorder in the Diagnostic Statistical Manual-IV in 1994, according to Dr. Martin Seligman, a proponent of positive psychology.

After 100 years of presenting conflicting, often confusing research theories on human sexuality, it remain uncertain as to why some people become heterosexual while others homosexual. The determinants of sexual orientation remain a mystery for now, according to social psychologist-authors Drs. D. Myers and & N. De Wall in 2016.

Conclusion

Sexual orientation is a very deep part of personal identity. It is a very stable personal characteristic. You cannot willfully choose or easily change your sexual orientation. It seems it chooses you. Discriminating against homosexuals is much like rejecting a person for being curly-haired or left-handed.

One significant finding though suggests that one's *first* feeling-of-erotic attraction basically defines one's sexual orientation. (*Sino ang 'unang' nagpatibok?*). Who triggered your "first" erotic attraction? inquired my grinning sex-guru kibitzer-friend.) Conversion from one orientation to another could be impossible, so we are told.

Sexology is a science, which is probably why it is so difficult to reconcile with religion (belief). Yet, Thomas Moore in one of his books wrote this sweet caveat: "Without sensuality, our religion becomes dry and aggressive. Without deep spirituality, our materialism grows hollow, unsatisfying, and compulsive."

It would be rare for everyone to agree on any one thing. As one Herbert Carrol once wrote almost a century ago, "The distant galaxies are more amenable to human understanding than human behaviors." Always, someone, somewhere, some Mike Pences will attempt to refute these words, quipped my androgynous kibitzer-friend.

You be the judge.

PH Mental Health Law: A bright beginning for Filipinos

By Dr. Aggie Carson-Arenas
Columnist, Inquirer, US Bureau, July 12, 2018

Dr. John Mackenzie spoke of a patient, Ms. P. who allegedly suffered from a "respiratory distress," we might dub today as asthma? Ms. P. professed that she was allergic to flowers, specifically roses.

On one occasion, Ms. P. came to see Dr. Mackenzie. As Ms. P. walked into the consultation-room, she noticed a huge bowl of roses on the table, took one look at the flowers… gasped, then went into a paroxysmal reaction: coughing; swollen nostrils; a tight chest.

The doctor led her into the treatment room; the nurse immediately gave her a hypodermic injection as she was wheezing heavily.

When Ms. P. stopped wheezing, she reproached the doctor, "How could you be so thoughtless, you know how sensitive I am to roses?!" Whereupon the doctor went toward the flower vase, snipped a "rose bud," and tore it into little pieces. It was a bouquet of *paper* roses!

He then whispered to Ms. P. that the injection given her was pure sterile water! (This obscure, but oft-cited case is attributed to John Mackenzie, a surgeon in Baltimore in the 1880s).

Was Ms. P.'s case purely medical, psychological, psychiatric, or mere ideational?

Atypical

Ms. P's case seems atypical, albeit from a clinician's perspective it does present us the general potential complexities in dealing with a *living* human being associated with one's mental, physical (or sometimes even spiritual) state of health.

"No longer shall Filipinos suffer silently in the dark. Mental health issues will now cease to be seen as an invisible sickness spoken only in whispers," said Senator Hontiveros, former chair of the Senate committee on health.

Hontiveros is the proponent of the newly signed Mental Health Law of the Philippines, or Republic Act 11036, which aims to give better access to mental health care among Filipinos. The law was signed on June 21, 2018.

The first Mental Health Act was filed three decades ago in 1989 by then Senator Orlando Mercado; there were at least 16 other bills before becoming a law.

The law seeks to provide mental health services down to the barangay level and integrate mental health programs in hospitals. It also seeks to improve mental health facilities and to promote and integrate mental health education in academe and workplaces.

A spokesperson for a coalition group jubilantly declared, "We say goodbye to taboo, superstition, and myths about mental health issues now that services are made accessible for all citizens... protects rights and welfare of people with mental health conditions, shifts focus of care to the community, improves access to services..."

Allocation

The World Health Organization (WHO) reported in 2007 that the Philippines spends about 5% of the total health budget on mental health, where substantial portions of which are spent on the operation and maintenance of mental hospitals. This means that only a marginal portion is allotted *directly* into patients' management.

However, with the new law, this would likely change. The total 2018 budget of the Department of Health (DOH), including budgetary support for government corporations, is Php171.09 billion (US$3.2 billion), according to Senator Legarda, chair of the Senate Committee on Finance.

The new law specifically states that the amount necessary for the initial implementation of the provisions of the law shall initially be charged against the current year's appropriations of the DOH. Thereafter, five percent (5%) of the incremental revenues from the excise tax on alcohol and tobacco products collected shall be earmarked (continually?) pursuant to Republic Act No. 10351.

The DOH has a broad mandate: formulate; develop; and implement a national mental health program based on the policy and objectives provision explicitly defined in the law. This author, Dr. Carson-Arenas advocates that this broad mandate be shared with the *Psychological Association of the Philippines* (PAP).

PAP is the largest collegial organization of mental health professionals, providers, and researchers' equivalent to that of the *American Psychological Association* (APA). PAP was founded in 1962, with the mission to "excellence in the teaching, research, and practice of psychology, and its recognition as a scientifically oriented discipline for *human* and *social development*."

Moreover, empirical studies suggest that many practitioners of healing estimate that 50% to 80% percent of patients who consult medical doctors suffer from *functional* disorders. Disorders of this kind are those thought to originate from the mind for which no organic or physiological basis can be established lucidly, demarcated or verified.

The rub

The Philippines has a population of 105.1 million with a ratio of human resources working in mental health at 3.5:100,000 where rates are particularly low for social workers and occupational therapists, reported WHO in 2007. Reports also show that currently there are 700 Filipino psychiatrists and a thousand psychiatric nurses practicing.

The rub is, out of the 700 psychiatrists, more than 50% work in for-profit mental health facilities and private practice. The distribution of human resources for mental health tends to favor that of mental health facilities in urban areas; far-flung places are often left without any mental health assistance.

The Mental Health Atlas of WHO reported a decade ago that the number of psychiatrists per 100,000 of the general populations is like the majority of countries in the Western Pacific region, which is about *average for lower middle resource countries.*

This is probably acceptable in the Philippines if the number is equitably distributed. The seven hundred psychiatrists would not even suffice if we "equally" allocated one Filipino psychiatrist per island in an archipelagic country of 7,107 islands (during low tide, quips a kibitzer friend).

We are reminded that studies show one in five Filipino suffers from some sort of a mental health problem or issues. The National Statistics Office (NSO) reported in 2016 that 88 cases of mental health issues were reported for every 100,000 Filipinos, a conservative estimation or number that is probably reflective of the more *profound* conditions.

Moreover, adding to the number of psychiatrists available; the number of psychologists practicing within the realm of mental health (clinical, developmental, educational, social, health, community, and forensic), and other allied mental health professionals or providers (social workers) could somehow alleviate this paucity of mental health professionals.

It should be also noted that the Filipino psychologists were 'professionalized' barely eight years ago upon the   passage of The Psychology Law of the Philippines or Republic Act No. 10029 on March 16, 2010.

Are psychologists now at par — "professionally" — with psychiatrists? The contention remains, unless the precise pathological cause is lucidly, resolved.

Meaning, if the cause-and-effect remains "*purely*" psychological, it's a psychologist's domain, quips my psych-kibitzer friend.

We are forewarned: The role played by physicians, psychiatrists, and psychologists in mental health is not devoid of controversies which, my *balimbing* (turncoat) kibitzer friend quips would be another interesting topic of its own to write about as hinted in Ms. P.'s case.

Advocates

Before the Philippine Mental Health Law was finally signed, advocates cried that, the country had gargantuan mental health problems. The truth is this is the same sentiment or tone echoed even among developed countries.

Different Filipino groups, coalitions, and organizations used to clamor that, "Aside from cases of psychiatric conditions, there's the lack of mental health professionals, facilities, funding, and a national law."

Filipinos now have the Mental Health Law. Where do we start?

Maybe in the doorsteps of the academe…"where the Filipinos are still *developing beings* who are in a unique, often precarious, relatively short phase of human development within a delicately prescribed timeframe…"

One bitter-sweet caveat arises though: As with any new law, the bigger challenge lies in the implementation. Advocacy never stops, it only pauses.

*In quo et nos incipere?**

*But where we could begin?

Psychology of siesta

By Dr. Aggie Carson-Arenas
Columnist, Inquirer, U.S. Bureau, June 25, 2021

It is estimated that *reduced productivity* or economic output due to insufficient sleep is costing U.S. businesses an average of about $345.50 billion a year according to a 2017 survey. This was only $18 billion per reported by industrial and organizational psychologists (I/O psychologist) in 2000.

This productivity lost is currently about PhP14 trillion, or *four* times the Philippines' approved national budget of PhP4.100 trillion for the fiscal year 2020 (rate of exchange at 48.7711/US$1).

Siesta is simply a 'rest.' A pause. It is basically a *nap*, usually taken after the midday meal (at least among Filipinos). Empirical studies suggest that the Spaniards clandestinely brought *siesta* besides their cross and the sword, which however seems undepicted on historical records quips my aspiring *historia*-somnologist kibitzer friend.

Did the people of the *Islas de Ponienta* (Island of the West), the pre-Filipinos of this era practiced *siesta*? Three-hundred-thirty-three years of colonization indeed, we did. The remnant of this practice is still observable among a majority of Filipinos today.

Is siesta really a *mere* national pastime? Most would remember as children in the Philippines that siesta was strictly imposed by adults during noontime. This was to 'get rid' of us for a while than anything else for them to enjoy the stillness of the noon to siesta.

Is *siesta* a good or a bad habit?

Habit

Empirical studies suggest that napping or *siesta* has a long history in many cultures, however America dismissed the habit during the Industrial Age as a timewaster. Many westerners associate siesta with indolence among those who practice it.

A Mexican snoozing complete with a huge *sobrero*, a colorful poncho unmindful of passerby against a backdrop of cacti is ascribed to be a sign of laziness. Even in the Philippines, *batugan* (sloth) is the colloquial term for those who seems to catch more than forty winks.

There are books on the market about napping like The *Arts of Napping at Work* by Anthony, W.A & Anthony, C. W., and *Power Sleep* by Dr. Maas, J. B., we are told. A book about the arts of napping? Filipinos were trained on napping for 333 years when colonized by Spain, quips my barriotic kibitzer friend.

Trend

Sleep was thought 'scientifically' studied as early as 1897 by Sigmund Freud who however dealt more on the *contents* of dreams during sleep than sleep per se. Dr. Dement, W. C. was one of the pioneering psychologists who studied sleep, dream, and with much focus on sleep deprivation during the 1976s. Dr. Dement was the founding president of the American Academy of Sleep Medicine (AASM).

Dr. Dement studied *sleep deprivation* among respondents who were kept awake for stretches as long as 200 hours continuously. This is equivalent to more than eight sleepless days!

Respondents reported experiencing weariness, lack of concentration, a decline in creativity, irritability, and a tendency toward hand tremors while being kept awake. This could be bad news to professions or industries where "sleep interruption or deprivation" is the rule of thumb.

Studies show that sleep deficiency or "lack of sleep" appears to be most common among protective services (police, EMC, firefighters) and the military; medical or health support (doctors and nurses); transportation and material transport (utility and drivers), and; production and retail (graveyard shift workers).

"This is disconcerting because many of these occupations are related to population health, well-being and safety services," according to the AASM report. Most of these occupations or industries involve long hours often with 'unpredictable' shifts.

Empirical studies reveal that sleep is directly related to daytime performance, productivity and well-being. According to the National Institute of Health (NIH) getting sufficient sleep show greater alertness, faster reaction times, better problem-solving and increased creativity in well- rested workers. Which are all positive attributes needed to work safely, healthy and productively.

Nevertheless, the good news is that after being able to regain normal sleep once again, sleep-deprived bounces back quickly, concluded Dr. Dement. This means 'recouping' with lack of sleep is possible. Just having twice, the amount of sleep one gets in a normal night enables one to perform at pre-deprivation levels.

However, with technological and entertainment indulgences, 'recouping' is negated or outrightly put aside quips my fun-loving kibitzer friend.

Self-employed workers register to have the lowest rate of sleep-deprivation; this is apparently because most are able to set their own schedules

After almost half a century, American businesses are heeding the message about the value of well-rested employees. A number of companies have incorporated napping facilities into their workplaces and some airlines and trucking companies now allow supervised siestas according to an article in the *Psychology Today* as early as the 1998.

The rub is, currently doctor and nurses are *still* being tasked to duty 12, to 16 hour straight-shifts. Graveyard shift schedules could be as erratic or insalubrious often more focus on the trends of economic supply and demand than individual need concern of the employees quips my I/O psychologist kibitzer friend.

Evidence

There is scientific evidence that napping may help one live longer according to 2012 studies. A recent study with 24,000 participants suggests that those who regularly nap are 37% less likely to die from heart disease than occasional nappers are. Researchers suggest naps maintain the heart's stress hormones down.

Will napping regain legitimacy because it makes employees feel better and be *officially* recognized as a productivity booster? According to Dr. Clark, F. C. Director of Labor and Employment Relation at the PennState, "… the sudden vogue for dozing is hurried Old World lifestyle, but a very American effort to get employees to work harder and more productive once they wake up."

Moreover, one economic benefit derived claims a California consulting firm many years ago in allowing workers to sleep on the job was that since it set up a nap room, its expenditures on caffeinated soda and coffee have dropped 30%.

Finally, to nap or not to nap *officially* is your own decision. Just don't let your guard down to make sure the stigma of "*batugan*" equated with *siesta* does not appear on your performance record.

Can hazing be stopped once and for all?

By Dr. Aggie Carson-Arenas
Columnist, Inquirer, US Bureau, May 11, 2017

The harshest law won't scare fraternity members into stopping the practice of hazing. No one, not even Presidents Trump and Duterte, or the head of the United Nations, can stop initiation rite deaths in universities. It's all part of human nature; it's rooted in psychology.

Various institutions (and disciplines) have called for an end to hazing, calls often triggered by abuses committed during the activity. The latest event is the "permanent banning of the Beta Theta Pi fraternity from Penn State, and strict new rules for Greek organizations on campus."

This was triggered by the death of Timothy Piazza, a 19-year-old student who died because his "own friends failed to get help for him for many hours"; Piazza fell multiple times down a stairway after consuming toxic levels of alcohol during a fraternity rite.

"Heart-wrenching and incomprehensible – 18 fraternity members charged," according to the *Washington Post*. A glimpse into the psychology of hazing would show why hazing is a seasonal-vicious-cycle.

Greek-letter societies

Hazing, simply defined, is initiation by exacting humiliating performances on the newbie or a would-be member of a group, from playing rough practical jokes or physical abuse that could lead to more grim consequences.

On a winter night, Frederick Bronner, a California junior college student, was taken 3,000 feet up and 10 miles into the hills of a national forest. Left to find his way home, wearing only thin sweatshirt and slacks, Fat Freddy, as he was called, shivered in a frigid wind until he tumbled down a steep ravine, fracturing bones and hurting his head. Due to sustained injuries, he huddled there against the cold, dying of exposure.

At Kappa Sigma house, University of Southern California (USC), the eyes of 11 pledges bulged when they saw the sickening task before them. Eleven-quarter pounds of raw liver lay on a tray. Thick cut and soaked in oil, each was to be swallowed whole, one to a boy. Gagging and choking repeatedly, young Richard Swanson failed three times to down his piece. A determined pledge, he finally got the oil-soaked meat into his throat where it lodged and, despite all efforts to remove it, choked him to death.

A pledge of Zeta Beta Tau fraternity was taken to a beach area of New Jersey and told to dig his "own grave." Seconds after he complied with orders to lie flat in the finished hole, the sides collapsed, suffocating him before his prospective fraternity brothers could dig him out.

Rite of passage

Hazing is meant to be a "rite of passage," a transition from one stage to another often marked by a ritual or ceremony entailing basic human behavioral follies.

It seems incomprehensible that students blessed with so much material and intellectual abundance would willingly and happily conspire to inflict pain on a friend through hazing. Fraternity rites are often brutal, mimicking primitive practices.

In Tonga for instance, a boy is required to go through an elaborate initiation ceremony before he is counted as a *man-member* of the tribe. He has to endure a great deal of pain and suffering. The hazing mystery could be rooted in this practice. This initiation is a three-month ceremonial ordeal, depicted several decades ago by anthropologists Whiting, Kluckhohn, and Anthony:

When a boy is somewhere between 10 and 16 years of age, his parents send him to "circumcision school," which is held every four to five years.

The initiation begins when the boy runs a gauntlet, two rows of men who beat him with clubs. His clothes are stripped, and he is made bald at the end of the rite.

He is next met by a man covered with lion manes, seated upon a stone. As he faces this "lion man," someone from behind strikes him; when he turns his head to see the striker, his foreskin is seized, cut off in two movements by the "lion man." He is afterward secluded for three months in the "yard of mysteries," where only the initiated could see him.

During the course of his initiation, the boy undergoes six major trials: beating; exposure to cold; thirst; eating of unsavory foods; punishment; and the threat of death, all quite similar to contemporary fraternity hazing practices.

Irony

Many have the impression that members of Greek-letter societies are composed of psychological or social miscreants whose twisted minds demand to be gratified with some sadistic-sociopathic acts inflicted on another human being.

However, the evidence shows otherwise. A study conducted by C. S. Johnson a few decades ago showed that "the personality traits of fraternity members show them to be, if anything, slightly healthier than other college students in their psychological adjustment."

Moreover, "members become aberrantly harsh as a group at only one time: immediately before the admission of a new pledge to the fraternity." The evidence thus seems to point to the ceremony itself as the culprit, where some kind of collective rigor vital to the group inexplicably comes to the fore.

Unstoppable?

In the Philippines, a law was enacted in 1995 classifying death due to hazing as a heinous crime; meaning anyone found guilty of it can be meted life imprisonment. Have these deterred would-be-hazing practitioners? Not at all, it seems.

Various institutions and administrations have tried threats, social pressures, legal actions, banishment, bribes and bans to persuade or even coerce groups to remove hazards and humiliations from their initiation ceremonies. None has been successful.

Many American colleges have tried to eliminate dangerous practices by taking direct control of the initiation rites. Fraternities do not only slyly circumvent such attempts, but they are also often met with outright physical resistance.

In the aftermath of Richard Swanson's choking death at USC in 1988, the university president issued new rules — requiring school authorities review all pledging activities and that adult advisers be present during initiation ceremonies. According to one national magazine: "...The new 'code' set off a riot so violent, that city police and fire detachments were afraid to enter campus."

How effective will be the "permanent banning of the Beta Theta Pi fraternity from Pennsylvania State, and strict new rules for Greek organizations on campus?"

Quo Vadis?

The 18 fraternity members charged in Penn State hazing death may all be proven guilty, expelled, tried and go to prison; will this halt hazing among groups of men?

Hazing is a universal activity, and every bit of evidence points to this conclusion that no one will likely be able to ban it effectively. Refuse to allow it openly and it will go underground. You cannot ban sex, prohibit alcohol (and now cannabis), and you likely cannot eliminate hazing.

Hazing is a rite of passage. It is a human folly, which is an integral part of human behavior. We are reminded that "the distant galaxies are more amenable to scientific study than is human behavior."

It's about time to deal with kids' mental health in schools

By Dr. Aggie Carson-Arenas
Columnist, Inquirer, US Bureau, June 24, 2018

"Mom, I'm gonna kill myself. I can't take it anymore. I just want to die. I want to go to the woods and kill myself. Can you just leave me on the road somewhere?'

Gianni, nearly five years old boy, said this an hour after being prescribed an untested antidepressant by a doctor, who did not know exactly what was wrong with him.

"You're so desperate you're willing to take anything as a diagnosis," Gianni's mother recalls that episode in a 2011 CNN report. Is Gianni bad, disturbed, or ill? What can be done to help youngsters like him?

Neuropsychiatric disorders in children could swell by 50 percent by 2020, putting them among the five leading causes of childhood illness, disability and death, according to the World Health Organization (WHO).

Many experts admit inability to explain precisely why mental issues among children are rising rapidly. Is it related to increased stress in children, families, "social disintegration" or a remarkable level of insecurity among young people?

Wanted: Early intervention

Complex psychological symptoms, abnormal behaviors, impaired functioning, or any combination of these often characterizes mental disorders. This is what experts mainly agree on: Early interventions prevent or mitigate onset of mental disorder.

Early intervention means early assessment; missing the early warning signs or aberrations during childhood or adolescence means losing the *intervention opportunity* and could lead to more serious mental disorder later in adulthood.

Half of all mental health disorders show first signs before the age of 14, and three quarters of mental issues begin before age 24. Despite state and private insurance programs, less than 20 percent of mental health problems receive needed treatment.

Chronic childhood adversity, now recognized more far more prevalent than researchers had imagined, could lead to mental issues. These childhood experiences include an incarcerated family member, an unexpected or untimely death in the family, depression, violence, abuse or drug use in the home, or periods of homelessness.

Unfortunately, the education system often responds bluntly to children manifesting mental challenges. Many academic personnel resort to traditional disciplinary measures from yelling and "timeouts" to detentions and suspensions. These only enhance stress, are ineffective and make things worse for many students.

Barriers, solutions

The US Surgeon General reported, "One in five Americans experiences a mental disorder in any given year. Unfortunately, half of those with severe mental illness do not seek treatment."

There are subtle barriers to accessing mental treatment: stigma or embarrassment is associated with mental illness; shortage of providers, long seen as significant problem in the U.S.; lack of information; parents themselves burdened with mental issues, are, among others.

Reforms to help reduce crime, incarceration and homelessness have been proposed as solutions. Newer concepts are also emerging.

Providing care through patient-centered medical homes into which many community clinics are now morphing is one. These facilities integrate mental, medical, vision and dental care so patients can seek treatment for a range of disorders under one roof. This integration resolves an array of barriers, thus optimizing each service.

"Screening students" and "teaching emotion" in school are also proposed. These, however, are not without controversies flaring up among parents, providers and school administrators.

Screening in schools

"Mental health screening can save lives," contended advocacy-group Mental Health America (MHA) in 2013. "Thanks to the results of research and technology, our mental health can be measured much like other vital signs in our body, such as heart rate or blood sugar, stated, Wayne W. Lindstrom, Ph.D., president and CEO of MHA.

"Screenings for mental health are just as important as school and sport physicals," according to Laurie Glynn, executive director of the TeenScreen National Center for Mental Health Checkup at Columbia University.

Early widespread screening in the middle school to identify struggling children has been proposed. A bill first introduced in 2007 (H.R. 1211: Mental Health in Schools Act of 2015) went to congressional committee in March 2015.

Teach 'emotion' in classroom

"Every classroom in America, starting as early as kindergarten, should begin each morning by placing magnetized name tags next to a 'How I Am Feeling' chart — a pledge of personal allegiance that tells teachers, fellow students, and parents that it's okay to be sad, angry, and happy," suggested columnist Clark Young.

"Teachers should then record that daily information in a personal, morning journal to discover patterns of expression that may result in the need for further understanding alongside parents, principals, and social workers. In this day and age, an email or text titled 'Today, your child says he/she is feeling…' could be sent to parents by 9:10 a.m.," added Young.

The goal is for children to understand their own anger, frustration, and sadness or what emotion they have for the day. In the immediate sense, red flags will become more accessible, and feelings easier to discuss. Relationships will develop. The rub is some school districts have a social worker to student ratio of 1:400.

Mental illness is a critical public health problem that must be addressed immediately. Besides expanding services and creating full-service schools there is a need for comprehensive, multi-faceted approaches that help make schools caring and supportive places that maximize learning and wellbeing and strengthen students, families, schools, and neighborhoods.

Advocacy or a crusade on mental health should begin at the doorsteps of the academes.

What we should know about teen suicide

By Dr. Aggie Carson-Arenas
Columnist, Inquirer, US Bureau, October 2, 2016

"In 2010 I was severely depressed, suicidal, and feeling like a failure at life, so I tried to kill myself – obviously, I was a failure at that too, thankfully," wrote Kathryn Hollander-Kidder, a teenager at that time. Was Kathryn's survival upon a first attempt at suicide typical?

Studies reveal that 60 percent of the completed suicides are successful on the first attempt; that the duration between suicidal thought and attempt is usually only about 10 minutes. This is why we cannot identify those who will commit suicide in the near future – we can only identify those with highest risk for potential suicide.

Studies suggest that suicide is rare in the young; it occurs with increasing frequency as adolescence advances, the second leading cause of death among teens or 15–29-year-olds globally in 2012. It is more frequent among the aged, in men, and among the single, isolated and widowed. It is one of the ten leading causes of death in most industrial countries.

Why did Kathryn attempt suicide knowing she had but one life to live? The answers could be varied as the cobblestones. One may simply call it stupidity while others may philosophically cite it as an ultimate challenge to God, or merely succumbing to physio-psychosocial issues.

Transient thoughts of death and dying are universal, and thoughts of self-destruction are frequent. How much control do we have over suicide is the sixty-four-thousand-dollar question.

Root

Mental health experts have long suspected that depression is the plinth to the cask of causing suicide. Depression is a state of despondency characterized by feelings of inadequacy, lowered activity, and pessimism about the future, which could be "typical" in normal individuals.

Medical studies have suggested two possible major types of depression, the *endogenous* and *exogenous* depressions.

Endogenous depression according to Fred Worshofsky, is "often hereditary; the suicide risk is greatest." The late Dr. Ian Skottowe of England's Wessex Regional School of Psychiatry explained, "It is quite especially morbid, not a mere intensification of normal experience."

Two origins of endogenous depression are identified–*predisposed* and *psychogenetic*. Predisposed depression is both physiological and psychological such as loss of appetite, weight, virility, sleep. Psychogenic depression on the other hand is usually caused by emotional or environmental factors where one often prompts a cry for help.

Exogenous depression is firmly rooted in trauma. Studies revealed that traumatic events could have consequences affecting subtly, or indelicately, feelings or behaviors; exactly what those consequences entail is sometimes necessarily not understood. Studies suggest that while the link between suicide and mental disorders is well established in high-income countries, many suicides happen impulsively in moments of crisis with a breakdown in the ability to deal with life stresses, such as financial problems, relationship break-up or chronic pain and illness.

Dr. Erwin Ringel, a Viennese psychiatrist and the founder of the International Association for Suicide Prevention, estimates that more than half the people (no estimate given for teens) who commit suicide contact a doctor before the attempt. "It is clear, that this is done in the hope that the doctor will stop them," reported Ringel.

Constellations

Dr. Igor Galynker, a contemporary expert on suicide prediction warned, "Sixty percent of the completed suicides are successful on the first attempt. We can identify those individuals with highest risk for potential suicide, but we cannot identify those who will commit suicide in the near future. In part, this is because the duration between the suicidal thought and attempt is usually only about 10 minutes."

There are myriad misconceptions relating to suicide, according to Dr. Barry N. Feldman, a prevention expert and currently director of psychiatric programs in public safety at the University of Massachusetts Medical School. "Neither bullying, pressure to succeed in sports or academics, nor minority sexual orientation can cause suicide, but are among a number of possible risk factors. If you focus too much on just bullying or sexual orientation, you take your eye off the underlying vulnerability a kid may have," said Feldman.

Suicide is typically caused by a constellation of risk factors and underlying vulnerabilities. "It is an attempt to solve a problem of intense pain with impaired problem-solving skills," again according to Dr. Feldman who proposed the acronym FACTS as a tool to outline the warning signs for teenage suicide: *Feelings* (helplessness, hopelessness); *Actions* (drug or alcohol abuse); *Changes* (in personality); *Threats*; *Situations* (getting into trouble).

Attempts at teen suicide prevention are not new. Suicide prevention centers, run mostly by ministers and laypersons with sympathetic ears, have been functioning in many countries for some years.

Suicide is one of the priority conditions in the WHO Mental Health Gap Action Programme (mhGAP) launched in 2008, which provides evidence-based technical guidance to scale up service provision and care in countries for mental, neurological and substance use disorders.

In the WHO Mental Health Action Plan 2013-2020, WHO Member States have committed themselves to working towards the global target of reducing the suicide rate in countries by 10 percent by 2020. Would the Mental Health Reform Act of 2016 make much difference?

Of Mass Shootings and mental Illness

By Dr. Aggie Carson-Arenas
Columnist, Inquirer, US Bureau, August 22, 2019

"Mental illness and hatred pull the trigger, not the gun," Trump said, addressing the nation after a weekend's mass shootings where 22 lives were lost in El Paso, Texas, another that left nine dead in Dayton.

For someone who consistently treats science and data as nuisances, or ignorable, pointing the finger at mental illness and hatred is convenient.

This idea may well be whirling inside his head: How it is possible that someone can randomly kill two dozen strangers and not be mentally ill ... can a healthy person do that?

A mental illness diagnosis is *not* always evidence of risk of violence toward other people. Fifty percent of Americans meet criteria for a mental illness at some point in their lifetime and most will not go on to commit violent crimes, according to Dr. McGinty, an associate professor at the Johns Hopkins Bloomberg School of Public Health.

Data

The American Psychiatric Association reported people with serious mental illness commit only about three (3%) percent of violent crimes. Thus, studies indicate only a minority of mass shootings have been perpetrated by individuals with recognized mental disorders, according to forensic psychiatrists Drs. Knoll IV and Annas.

Nevertheless, post hoc analyses indicate that perpetrators are full of rage and may harbor "fantasies of violent revenge" for real or imagined offenses against them; these may lie entirely beneath the surface until they put the fantasies into action. Such individuals wrote Drs. Knoll IV and

Annas, function in society and do not typically seek out mental health treatment.

In most cases, therefore, it cannot fairly be said that a perpetrator "fell through the cracks" (as the president was heard saying during his candidacy) of the mental health system. Rather, these individuals typically plan their actions well outside the awareness of mental health professionals, so we are told.

Most mental health symptoms examined, including anxiety, depression, stress, PTSD, and borderline personality disorder, were unrelated to gun violence, according to Dr. Yu Lu, a postdoctoral research fellow at the University of Texas Medical Branch. Moreover, the World Health Organization (WHO) also reported that neuropsychiatric disorders in children could swell by 50 percent by 2020.

The rub is experts remind us that individuals who conduct these acts very often do not see themselves as mentally ill whatsoever or in need of any treatment or intervention.

A study by Drs. Peterson and Densley reveals that there are commonalities among the perpetrators of nearly all the mass shootings they studied, including: a vast majority experienced early childhood trauma with early exposure to violence; everyone was at an identifiable crisis point prior to the shooting; most studied other shooters' actions and sought validation for their motives and had the means to carry out plans.

Adverse Childhood Experiences (ACEs) encompass the chronic, unpredictable, and stress-inducing events that some children face, which in the study specifically include parental suicide, physical or sexual abuse, neglect, domestic violence, and/or severe bullying. Trauma often leads to mental health issues such as depression, anxiety, thought disorders or suicidality.

Studies also show that half of all mental health disorders show first signs before the age of 14, and three quarters of mental issues begin before age 24. The rub is, only less than 20 percent of mental health problems receive needed treatment. The disheartening question: How many are under the ACEs clout?

APA president Dr. Rosie Davis forewarned that routinely blaming mass shootings on mental illness is unfounded and stigmatizing. The rates of mental illness are roughly the same around the world, yet other countries are not experiencing these traumatic events as often as we do. Adding racism, intolerance, and bigotry to the mix is a recipe for disaster.

Trigger

The other commonality is an identifiable crisis point prior to the shootings. Problematic substance use, especially of alcohol, is a major risk factor that could influence whether a person will use a gun to commit a violent crime (but not necessarily mass shooting?), reported the Consortium for Risk-Based Firearm Policy, an advocacy group for gun violence prevention; the alcohol problem often triggers or aggravates other real or ideational crises.

Mass shooters often are angry and despondent because of a specific grievance -- a change in job status and relationship rejection or loss often played a role. Such crises were, in many cases, according to Drs. Peterson and Densley, often subtly or sometimes explicitly conveyed to others through a distinct change in behavior, expression of suicidal thoughts or plans, or specific threats of violence.

Copycats

Human beings are susceptible to suggestion, and the mass media are the biggest source for spreading "affecting" information through 24/7 social media connectivity. It seems difficult to deny that the media coverage since the late '90s has made it certain that those who commit heinous crimes become "celebrities," noted Dr. Knoll IV.

The mantra is, my media-guru-kibitzer friend quipped, "you do not exist until you are a 'star' in social media."

Most shooters studied other shooters' actions and sought validation for their motives; a 'few' literally followed scripts that promised notoriety in death, according to Drs. Peterson and Densley. Perpetrators study other perpetrators and model their acts after previous shootings. Many are radicalized online in their search for validation from others that their will to murder is justified, perpetuating the copycat syndrome, so we are told.

Access

Having access to a gun is more of a risk factor for violence than being diagnosed with a mental illness, and individuals who have a history of risky or dangerous behavior are far more likely to commit gun violence than persons diagnosed with mental illness research shows, Kaitlin Sullivan reported in NBC.

In 80% of school shootings, perpetrators got their weapons from family members, a study indicates. Workplace shooters tended to use handguns they legally owned. Other public shooters were more likely to acquire them illegally. In one survey of inmates in state prisons who used guns to commit crimes revealed barely one in 10 had bought their own; the rest had begged, borrowed, or stolen guns.

Having access to a gun, coupled with 'certain personality traits,' is one such salient risk factor for gun violence. Individuals having access to a gun are more than 18 times as likely to threaten someone or attempt to harm others compared with those without gun access, according to a study in the journal of *Preventive Medicine*. If perpetrators had not been able to get guns, they could not have used them in their crimes.

Is 'Filipino' crab mentality a myth?

By Dr. Aggie Carson-Arenas
Columnist, Inquirer, U.S. Bureau, July 20, 2021

Filipinos are known for *utak talangka* or "crab mentality," for coming late to social events and for being *niñgas cogon* (a flash in the pan). However, social psychologists suggest that these social phenomena, attitudes, traits or attributes, or whatever your kibitzer friend wishes to call them, are *not* only evident among Filipinos but are actually prevalent among other races.

This article is *not* meant to offend or mock cultural frailties or flaws. It merely present *commonly* held cultural tendencies. Individual constitutions, not race must always prevail, insists my now-*naturalized* American citizen kibitzer friend.

What we think of as Filipinos-*lang* (only in the Philippines) are actually common among other groups. A Filipino American once wrote about his Jewish-couple friends constantly being tardy; it is not only a Filipino trait, but also a Jewish one called "Jewish Standard Time."

Any person who thinks he is of any importance wants to be fashionably late. It is an unwritten protocol or part of the "standard operating procedure" (SOP) for any VIP of *any* race to come late to social events. Everybody knows this as the "dramatic entrance." An eastern kibitzer friend admits for appointments, some Middle Easterners are the worst violators. It is acceptable not to show up at all!

"Crab mentality" or *utak talangka* is probably one of the more infamous and familiar sociocultural myths about the Filipino. *Talangka* is a variety of small local crab that my fisherman kibitzer friend identified as the *Asian shore crab*, which when a number are placed in a shallow container tend to escape, tugging/pulling down those ahead closer to the brim.

Empirical belief claims such mentality causes disunity, a hindrance to group success. A friend of a friend of my kibitzer friend confides that Fijians have the same problem, only ten times worse. Fijians are even afraid to say anything to another Fijian because an envious or jealous rumormonger may misrepresent — deliberately and maliciously — what another conveys.

Crab mentality is a social phenomenon that prevails in any society whether sophisticated or otherwise. Certainly, these get worse in celebrated political and corporate circles. In the top echelon of CEOs, presidents, or directors, "crabbing" is accepted and proudly equated with "gamesmanship" or political intrigue. This is true, from America to the Zulu islands, quips my Nigerian kibitzer friend.

This social phenomenon is also found in Australia, Canada, New Zealand and United Kingdom, where it is known as "tall poppy syndrome," in which an individual demonstrating *genuine merit* is resented, abused, or criticized simply because he is better than the rest!

Filipinos esteem "clannishness," which is why they are described as "factionalist." When a group shows promise and is thriving, it is likely that one or two members will "defect" to form another similar group. This, according to social scientists, is a global trait. That is why we have the term *ethnocentricity*, the belief that one's "own cultural" group is always superior to that of another.

Filipinos are so timid and reticent, saying "no" when they mean "yes," or "maybe" and vice versa. Yet, again, according to a bookworm kibitzer friend, there's an American book titled *How to Say No and Not*

Feel Guilty! Whether this attribute is indigenous to the Filipino or a mere residue of a colonial past is an open question. My historian kibitzer friend reminds us that the Philippines was colonized for 333 years.

Similarly, among Finns, timidity is expressed differently — even the extroverts are introverts. In Finland, expressed another kibitzer Finn, there's a saying, "An introverted Finn looks at his shoes when talking to you; an extrovert Finn looks at your shoes."

Another interesting trait, *ningas cogon*, which literally means 'cogon fire' (cogon is a tindery wild-grass common in the Philippines), refers to an intense enthusiasm for a task at the beginning, which soon fades away — a flash in the pan.

Pioneers of Filipino psychology the likes of Andres, Arjona, Batacan and Samson, suggested that this trait may be behind the failure of many projects.

The implementation of seatbelt-wearing comes to mind; it was welcomed at a certain time in the Philippines. Drivers seemed to follow this safety measure, according to statistical data. How many cities strictly implement this law today? Is it true that there is something that dampens everyone's compliance with such a simple life saving device?

Filipinos have been mislabeling themselves too long, depreciating themselves with a trait supposedly innate only to their race. "Filipino-*kasi*," is a frequent explanation when another Filipino misbehaves or commits an unbecoming act.

As Edward Wilmot Blyden once wrote, albeit in a different context, "The inspiration of the race is the race." Filipinos must stop the self-degradation.

'Manyakis': Moral and neural roots of sexual misbehavior

By Dr. Aggie Carson-Arenas
Columnist, Inquirer, US Bureau, Jun 21, 2018

Do you have to be filthy rich, famous, and powerful to be swept away by the current of the *@MeToo* phenomenon?

Dr. C is a widower, a typical fiftyish philosophy professor in a Catholic University, who for 20 years had been enthusiastically teaching philosophical ideas constantly infused with tons of moral virtues or ethics. Dr. C is soft-spoken, seldom smiles, and seems amiable most of the time.

He is a "famous" professor in the university *not* because of these attributes, but as the *manyakis* professor. "Manyakis" is Tagalog slang for "maniac," relating to the seemingly innocuous sexual advances or misconducts such as touching, stroking, rubbing, or kissing disguised as an accidental or innocent act.

These "accidental" acts are probably the *kinder* or subtle precursor triggers of today's @MeToo, which everybody took for granted for so many years. The perpetrators, as in the case of Dr. C, tended to be euphemistically dubbed as "fatherly."

If this university professor had the same vast power and fortunes like Harvey Weinstein could Dr. C's sexual behaviors been a lot of worst?

Perhaps.

Casting-Couch

It was journalist Ronan Farrow's pen that stirred the magma, spilling forth the @MeToo lava, revealing the sexual misconducts or offenses and scalding many, many privileged personalities and celebrities along the way.

All these started when media mogul Mr. W's libidinal practices were first exposed in *The New Yorker* by Farrow. Dr. C hasn't exposed.

There are about 2,350 therapists across the nation who provide court-mandated treatment to sex offenders; the rub is, "the" offense is often too difficult to identity or demarcate.

These therapists counsel in prisons and other government institutions based on state-authorized judges' referrals. Offenders have the option to see any private practitioners.

A sex offender according to Jennifer, a licensed professional prison counselor, often commits a crime by rationalizing it in some way: she wanted it; or my needs mattered more than hers. They convince themselves that a false notion is true — a cognitive distortion.

Mr. W apparently pleaded "not guilty" during his arraignment. Mr. W and his lawyers adamantly averred that every sexual encounter Mr. W had was consensual, although more than 50 women have made allegations against him publicly.

A piece written in 1937 by film critic and historian Carrie Rickey bluntly stated that moguls like Harry Cohn (co-founder of Columbia Pictures Corporation) reputedly would not cast starlets like Marilyn Monroe and Kim Novak unless they auditioned in bed.

This infamous practice is dubbed the Hollywood "casting-couch," which one of Mr. W's lawyers seemed to hint at as a defense tactic.

What pushes the relatively moralistic Dr. C, or filthy-rich Mr. W to let themselves be cast under the shadow of inappropriate sexual behaviors?

Vise versa

A "sexual misconduct," apparently equates to "inappropriate sexual behavior" and vice versa. Sexual misconduct is too vague a term, whereas *inappropriate sexual behavior* or ISB is now being admitted or at least recognized in the lexicon of psychology.

ISB is a relatively common and potentially disruptive form of behavior among geriatric people often with mental issues such as dementia that can cause distress and can put people at risk, according to Drs. Riccardo De Giorgi and Hugh Series of University of Oxford in their study.

In another related study, ISB is defined as a disruptive behavior characterized by a verbal or physical act of an explicit or perceived sexual nature, which is unacceptable within the social context in which it is conducted. Dr. Johnson of the Association for the Treatment of Sexual Abusers (ATSA) conducted the study.

In one other study conducted by Dr. Antonette M. Zeiss, former chief consultant for mental health at the Department of Veterans Affairs Central Office (VACO) and colleagues in 1996, the following were identified as ISB: sitting too close with another; arms or legs touching; kissing; stroking someone on the face hands, or arms; inappropriately undressing; rubbing up against another person; touching self on breasts or genitals in public; making explicit sexual comments; inappropriately touching someone; touching partner on breast or genitals in public; exposing one's breasts or genitals in public.

The word "*tiyansing*" comes to mind, Tagalog slang for "chancing," or subtle-seemingly-accidental-moves.

Another now familiar term, "sex addiction, "refers to a person with addictive or compulsive disorders, who frequently displays an inability to inhibit behaviors once he becomes maladaptive despite adverse consequences of his behavior, according to Dr. Lique Coolen of University of Mississippi Medical Center and colleagues.

These researchers specifically studied the role of the *medial prefrontal cortex* (mPFC) of the brain, the region associated with decision-making and behavioral flexibility. Non-human experiments identify mPFC as the potential mediator of behavioral inhibition.

Collectively these results suggest that sexual misconduct, ISB, and sex addiction tend to be neurological, i.e., entrenched in the brain.

Solution

In the 1980s, American states made the conclusion that *sex offenders were not sick, they were bad*, according to law professor John Q. LaFond, JD, of the University of Missouri-Kansas City. Some states decided to offer treatment, but there was not much hope that it would work.

Currently, however, there is an emerging optimism that mental health professionals can deal with these people and offer alternatives to continued incarceration, added LaFond.

One key consideration for both the gatekeepers of mental health and the gatekeeper of law is *timing*: the right person at the-right-intervention at the right time.

Timing is crucial, according to LaFond, to start therapy as soon as possible after incarceration. Offenders often fail to realize the severity of their crimes, and an antagonistic prison environment can exacerbate feelings of being wrongly accused and hamper treatment.

We are forewarned by LaFond that attitudes that led to offending can become stronger, more virulent in prison; offenders can develop explanations for themselves that become solidified over time. You want to confront erroneous ideas right away and make it clear that sex offenses are profoundly serious crimes.

However, the American Psychological Association (APA) reminds us that, people commit sexual crimes for distinct reasons. Dr. Aubrey of APA adds, "Some are highly predatory, highly psychopathic, and have repeated offenses, making them more likely to re-offend." There is the rub.

The sixty-four-thousand-dollar question remains: Are sex offenders sick, or are they bad? Could we exact a demarcation who is truly neurologically or morally flawed?

Your guess is as good as mine – so far.

Rizal the psychologist

By Dr. Aggie Carson-Arenas
Columnist, Inquirer, US Bureau, December 28, 2018

Once, two friends found a clam near the sea. They debated as to who should have it. "I," one said, "saw it first…;" "… but I picked it up," replied his friend. They went to court and asked the judge to settle the question.

The judge opened the shell, ate the meat, and divided the shell between the litigants.

This is an excerpt from *Rizal's Prose,* by the *Jose Rizal National Centennial Commission*, 1962, page 105, a witty reminder by a world-renowned Filipino national hero for those fond of resorting to the courts of justice.

Rizal's prose was tinged with both judicial and psychological contexts, but after 150 years is Rizal, with his idealism — reality molded by thoughts and ideas — still relevant today?

Dr. Jose Rizal was executed 124 years ago on the 30th of December 1896.

Irony

Rizal was truly a polymath, a polyglot who spoke several languages, a prolific writer and a European-trained ophthalmologist (probably the only one in the Far East during that era), yet Rizal seems not to have written anything about ophthalmology, his recognized profession.

The irony is that he had written a treatise entitled, "*The Cure of the Bewitched: Notes on the Study of Philippine Medicine*," expressly for

Benito Francia, the then-Inspector of Health. The article has something to do with *kulam* (witchcraft); quite unrelated to any ophthalmological ideas Rizal learned in Paris and Germany during his studies in 1885s to 1887s.

Rizal quoted studies, the most notable being a quarrel between a woman and a *manggagaway* (a female practitioner of *kulam* as Rizal himself distinguished from *mangkukulam* for male) where the former fell ill and died. The *manggagaway* received 50 lashes publicly, was thrown in jail where she committed suicide by hanging herself.

The bizarre twist of the case was that since part of the prison bars where the alleged "witch" hanged herself was too low, she would necessarily have had to fold her legs to commit "a successful" suicide. Defying their mediocre reasoning, the townsfolk readily explained this was a satanic-assisted act! The full account of this is written in the National Historical Commission, "*Iba't Ibang Sinulat Ni Rizal*," Vol. 8, 1961, page 93.

Voracious

Rizal's exile in Dapitan for four years and 14 days, from July 17, 1892, to July 31, 1896, was fruitful and serene, surmised some historians. According to Zaide, a famous Philippine historian, Rizal devoted all his time and efforts to the practice of medicine; his artistic, literary, educational, linguistic and scientific pursuits; his agricultural and business activities; certain civic projects; and his extensive correspondences with world-renowned scientists and personalities of that epoch.

Moreover, Rizal was a voracious reader. Rizal library included *Harriet Beecher Stowe's Uncle Tom's Cabin*; *Hebrew Grammar*; and *Lives of Presidents of the United States; The Byzantine Empire,* among others. His library also included several French books that dealt with hypnotism, experimental psychology and even clinical and therapeutic research on epilepsy, hysteria, neuroses and mental conditions.

Through his writings, Rizal attempted to dispel the superstitious beliefs in *kulam* during his time. One contemporary writer/columnist wrote, "Rizal not only gave us data useful to the folklorists and anthropologists, but he actually explained the route of treatment psychologically."

In other words, Rizal who likely was trained in the allopathic medicine, which is based entirely on a mechanistic theory of diseases and treatments recognized and accepted as the "scientific standard" of the day. Yet, in 1895 or more than a century and a half ago, Rizal seemingly veered from this "standard" when he argued that *kulam* was a mere product of suggestion, not sorcery.

His writings revealed that ailments could be alleviated without recourse to talisman or *agimat*, "strange" potions (e.g., *gayuma*), *oracion* or *dasal* (ritual or prayer), body-lashing with rattan, indigenous leaves or even *buntot pagi* (stingray tail, whip) where the victim seems unscathed while the *magkukulam* "bears" the pain, sometimes leading to death, bringing to mind the movie "The Exorcist."

Accolade

The search for the still-elusive "Filipino psychology," could have been started by Rizal sharing the idea that disease was attributable to these factors: air (*hangin*); heat (*init*); cold (*lamig*); and vapor from the earth (*singaw*) — the common belief of the period. Any "other condition" was ascribed to sorcery or *kulam*. Could Rizal have been the *"Father of Filipino Psychology* too? If only he had expounded his treatise.

Nevertheless, Rizal is thought to be the "father of the community school" in the Philippines when he established a school attended by 16 pupils, select boys from prominent families in Dapitan. There were no tuition fees, according to Epistolario Rizalina (Zaide, 1881: 192). Students were taught gardening and construction projects for the community.

Rizal indeed knew some basic principles of psychotherapy as well. This was manifested lucidly in his article "*Ang Paggamot Sa Mga Nakukulam*," (Treatment for the Bewitched/Hexed) found in the same source mentioned earlier.

Boredom

Rizal was probably bored during his exile in Dapitan of more than four years, enabling him to write on a staggering variety of subjects, articles mostly written in Dapitan included: "*The Sense of the Beautiful*" ; "*Suan's Animals*;" "*Reminiscences of a Cock*" (all translated into Spanish by Encarnacion Alzona on November 15, 1957; August 16, 1957; and March 10, 1959, respectively). "*The Kite and the Hen*;" "*The Fisherman and the Fish*" (both translated by Alzona from the French on March 12, 1959, and February 25, 1959); and "*A Reminder to those Fond of Lawsuits*".

Is Rizal's idealism still relevant today?

We are reminded that Rizal was 18 years old when he wrote, "*A La Juventud Filipina (To the Filipino Youth)*," where the oft-quoted phrase, "*Ang kabataan ang pag-asa ng bayan* (The youth is the hope of the fatherland)" is ingrained. Pepe, dedicated this poem to the youths of his time, winning him first prize in a poetry contest.

What *idealism* was reflected by an 18-year-old-Pepe in an era so different from ours? Rizal delved into parapsychology or the "paranormal" as early as a century and a half ago when pockets of revolts against a colonizer was the main course of the day.

What other subjects would Rizal have delved into if his life had been spared in Bagumbayan when he was only 35?

To observe or not to observe etiquette

By Dr. Aggie Carson-Arenas
Columnist, Inquirer, US Bureau, December 20, 2017

Are manners out of style these days? I am who I am.

Trump is Trump. Duterte is Duterte.

These statements imply, "I am a true, sincere person. This is me." Are these self-proclaimed actuations worth their salt?

Good manners are always in style. They change with demographics and time, but they never disappear according to Dana May Casperson, author of *Power Etiquette.*

People think, mistakenly, that etiquette means you have to suppress your individual differences, lose your unique individuality, or intentionally re-brand yourself.

Gregarious being

Etiquette is all about human social behavior. It is a little social contract we agree on to restrain some of our more provocative impulses, in return for living harmoniously in a community, according to Judith Martin, journalist, author and etiquette authority.

No one can be "sincere" forever only to oneself. Not even a president unless he is a non-gregarious being.

"I don't care about etiquette" simply denotes a lack of understanding about etiquette, confusing etiquette with non-conformism.

Others erroneously think etiquette as some kind of ritual for snobs. The rub is, when you throw etiquette away, injurious behavior and even violence can follow, e.g., road rage.

Yet, learning the "rules" of etiquette is easy. It's 80 percent common sense and 20 percent kindness.

Costs nothing

Today, we truly need etiquette back. The whole country, all of humanity, needs civility. Why don't we have it? It does not cost anything. No funding, no legislation involved. It is all commonsense and kindness.

The willingness to restrain oneself is one solution. Imagine if people only tweeted their thoughts politely. Some people want other people to be polite to them, but they insist on the freedom to be impolite to others. Civility does not work that way.

Civility requires some training in restraint, similar perhaps to the "delayed gratification" studied by Walter Mishel through his famed *marshmallow challenge* test among four-year-old-children in the '60s, to identify who may succeed or fail in future life. Would this work with seventyish men? Apparently, it could.

Attitude

Etiquette is all about harmoniously relating to others. It is the art of dealing with others, armed with a correct attitude. Positive attitudes exist in everyone's psyche. Attitude is a personality trait we continue to develop through life.

According to social psychologists Martin Fishbein and Icek Ajzien, attitude is a learned, relatively enduring pre-disposition to respond in consistently favorable or unfavorable ways to certain people, groups, ideas, or situations.

Parents should be teaching etiquette early in a child's life. "Darling, now do not pull the dog's tail. How would you feel if the dog pulled your tail?" If the kid retorts, I do not have a tail, so what do I care?" the teaching clearly needs to begin.

Formal education seldom includes much training in proper etiquette, experts remind us, and some recommend it should be an integral part of the academe. We learn manners from our family, friends and colleagues.

Manners are skills that need constant practice and updating. To observe or not to observe etiquette is an individual choice, unless of course one has some kind of psychopathological issue. Tweet that.

Sexual happiness beyond Valentine's Day

By Dr. Aggie Carson-Arenas
Columnist, Inquirer, US Bureau, February 2, 2018

Sexual happiness is a natural state, according to Dr. D. R. Butler, an obscure doctor-author this author read a decade or so ago. It is part of our birthright and not something achievable or attained by superhuman efforts. Sexual happiness just is it is part of our inner nature to honor and enjoy.

The irony is that a vast majority of people seems to be searching for sexual happiness. This is often the case regardless of how "together" couples seem to be in their heads; sexual happiness somehow eludes them.

One thing is certain: sexual happiness is elusive when we try to search for it. A truism that seems not easy to understand; this simply means that when we are searching for something, we obviously think we do not have it.

We are reminded that happiness, even sexual happiness, does not exist "out there" in the world somewhere. It does not come from others, not even from the one we love. Happiness exists within us, only waiting for its discovery.

Happiness is an outgrowth of bliss.

Napoleon Hill and W. Clement Stone in their book Success Through a Positive Mental Attitude write, "One of the surest ways to find happiness for yourself is to devote your energies toward making someone else happy."

"Happiness is an elusive, a transitory thing, and if you set out to search for it, you will find it evasive. But if you try to bring happiness to someone else, then it comes to you," added these authors. The halo of reciprocity brings a miracle when two individuals meet in these criteria.

Experts from time-to-time claim that the main reason happiness is so rare is because people are too accustomed to their unhappiness. Studies show that making others happy will draw one's own happiness from within, and it will increase and expand the more one shares it with another.

Still, in reality, we are hounded by sexual worries.

Sexual worries

As people grow older, they are liable to develop unnecessary worries about their sex lives. In fact, it is common for many marriages to be disrupted for sexual reasons in all levels of society.

However, the Sex Information Education Council of the United States and the National Institute of Aging, report that most people continue to enjoy sex throughout their life. The exceptions are usually found in those with some sort of physical disabilities, those who think they should not (for example, because of a previous medical issue), those who simply cannot and those who choose to remain celibate.

Generally, the major spoilers of sex for both among young and older people are alcohol, drugs, stress, strain and ignorance; the latter, often based on inaccurate information or mere ideation.

Below is a composite of excerpted ways from numerous studies to avoid such worries:

Every individual has his own *biorhythm*. Everyone is unique. Every sexual relationship has its vicissitudes; we must not judge it by its lowest moments. We must instead focus on the experiential state itself. There are occasions when environmental factors take their toll on us as we shall glean later.

Comparing has a price. We must not engross ourselves with information that frequently specifies an "average" sex life. There is no "pattern" to live up to. In other words, we should *not* compare ourselves with others that may only deflate our own ego because there will always be greater "statistical numbers" distinguishing us from the rest.

Never rely on "common knowledge" or accept everything as fact. These refer especially to ideas or "suggestions" conveyed by our neighbors, friends or colleague after hearing from "a-friend-of-a-friend," or online. When in doubt, confirm such information or data with authoritative books or experts.

Lead a well-balanced life and keep in the best physical condition you can. Worries often develop because of a too idle or narrow lifestyle. The more active and varied the activities in our life, the less chances of us being beset by worries. Physical prowess is best explored when fit; surely men know what this means.

It should be noted that while most healthy men continue to be sexually active all their lives, some do lose interest due to lack of practice. The dictum "use it or lose it" applies. Note also that male fertility can continue into extreme old age. Men in their nineties have fathered children, studies reveal.

Relationship

Studies also show that sex is not everything in a relationship. A marriage is not going to fall if it is not always at peak level. Sexual activity may wax and wane at certain times due sometimes too apparent or too inexplicable reasons. Our desire may occasionally dim due to stress or strain, but passion per se need not die.

When our sexual relationship loses some of its early zest, experts advise us not to worry that we are not satisfying our mate. Note that as we have matured, so has our mate — his or her sexual "caliber" is likely to be the same as ours. Nature constantly calibrates the thrill and joy among long-lasting relationships.

There are changes in our lives genetically defined as part of the aging process; some of which we cannot naturally prevent, delay or reverse. To understand their cause-effect, we must learn to identify whether what is affecting our zest is biological, mere ignorance, or simply imaginary.

Caveat

There are times when no matter how unwarranted they are, sexual worries can persist and build up in our minds. Talk them over with your mate and clear them up. There are times when an expectation simply remains because it is perhaps taken for granted.

There is one salient caveat: we are cautioned never to discuss our own sexual worries with just anybody — they may make our problems seem greater than they are. In exceptional cases, it may be wise to consult a professional regarding our problem.

Many times, our sex worries have nothing to do with sex at all.

Oftentimes these are mere growing concerns about our overall relationship with our mate. The children are just too rowdy. Perhaps the neighbor's dog is straying too often too long in our front yard, and we hate it; maybe we have a too-routinized-lifestyle, or perhaps the visit of our parents-in-law has lengthened.

In such instances, the best way to prevent sexual worries is by keeping up a warm, "total" relationship. We have the option to simply close our eyes, breathe deeply and count the bliss rather than the blues. Or console ourselves by this current survey: 57 percent of those in (even) unhappy relationships still find their partners extremely attractive.

Sex is a birthright we can enjoy for the rest of our life

Can 'standardized tests' impinge on our right to education?

By: Dr. Aggie Carson-Arenas
Columnist, Inquirer, U.S. Bureau. September 8, 2021

"America has been obsessed with student standardized tests for nearly 20 years," reported V. Strauss in her *Washington Post* piece, "It looks like the beginning of the end of America's obsession with student standardized tests," in 2020.

The Philippines ended this pernicious education obsession after 21 years — as early as 1994 quips an educational psychology kibitzer friend.

Who could forget the NCEE. It was during the Marcos regime in 1973 that the National College Entrance Examination or NCEE was implemented in the Philippines. This was a government-led standardized examination that must be taken by every graduating high school students — the gate to Higher Education.

This era was probably the most stressful era for most Filipino adolescent students aspiring to enter college. NCEE was the key, thought of as the final-one-shot-deal to hurdle before a student formally leaves high school. Failing to show up at the precise moment for whatever reason; you are done quips a kibitzer friend.

The NCEE ostensibly claimed to present *equal opportunity* for student migrants coming from far-flung regions of the Philippine, so we were told by the then regime. Many in the academe, however, believed this was to subtly force the millions of non-passers towards the path to vocational courses.

Vocational course enrolments during that epoch was pathetically marginal; has this changed after three decades? Others nevertheless thought NCEE was intended to *disrupt* the obsessive mindset of parents to "college-only-education" for their children, quips an education doctorate kibitzer friend.

Was the NCEE a wise a move? Was the NCEE research-based, or a mere whim of armchair experts or purely for political optics of the time? Or a Kronos' scythe that decimated dreams and hopes?

Can a standardized test impinge on our birthright to education?

Thrive

Parents will learn *nothing* from a child's test score (standardized), expressed Dr. D. Ravitch, a former U. S. Assistant Secretary of Education as part of her advocacy on educational testing. Parents really do not care about comparative rank results through bevy of numbers and data.

Parents simply want to know, whether their children are keeping up with their assignments, participating in class, understanding their school work, doing projects, enthusiastic about school activities, and having a good relationship with their teachers and peers.

"The standardized tests won't answer any of these questions. So, how can a parent find out what he or she wants to know? Ask your child's teacher," bluntly added Dr. D. Ravitch.

There's the rub. The Teacher. The biggest white elephant in every classroom, quips a nursery doctorate teacher kibitzer friend. Who then should write the test's contents?

Content

The teacher should write test's content based on what was taught in class. The teacher gets instant feedback and knows precisely what each student understood, what was not. A teacher can confer with a student to go over what was missed in class and help him learn what he needs to know, suggested Dr. Ravitch.

Experts remind us that tests fundamentally measures two things: what you know and/or what you do not know. Which is more important? It depends on the purpose of the test according to Mr. G. Vitamanti, a retired teacher from California who also writes for *The San Diego Union-Tribune.*

Cognitive scientists forewarn us that we do not know more than we do know. This is true, even among doctors or experts or scientists in any field; no human is omniscient. Herein lays the problem with state or national tests, wrote Vitamanti.

Empirical studies indicate that the people who dream up the test questions decide what is important from their point of view. Not only is this like having one political party, but it is also difficult to understand the objectives of the test makers.

The result is that students faced with answering questions they have never been exposed to, or which are irrelevant.

Departmentalized examinations have also become an integral part of many higher education systems. Should we not be wary of any test given to a student that one has not had a hand in constructing, inquired quizzically a cognitive psychologist kibitzer friend.

Uniformity is essential in departmentalization. Vitamanti averred, "Unless every teacher is given the same materials and the same lesson plans with exact guidelines as to what is most important – and therefore what the state or national test will cover – most of the students will start at a great disadvantage.

This means, many students may have not necessarily learned what will be on the test. To a great degree, it becomes a crapshoot."

Focus

This brings to mind a study on how students tackle problems, conducted a few decades ago by Dr. D. Laurillard now with the University College London. This probably is not much different from the idea on how to tackle a question relative to answering standardized test.

Dr. Laurillard's finding: The focus of learners' attention was not on the problem itself, but on the problem as set by a teacher in the context of a particular course. The idea of learning the concept simply dissolved or significantly negated.

The student's attentions were not focused on tackling the problem; rather on what they thought the teacher required, or in this instance, what the test would cover. The focal point therefore becomes simply: "Is this what the teacher is looking for?"

These simply means that the focus is on the answers rather than analyzing and fathoming the concept! Could this be the reason why "'review' facilities" (brick-and-mortar or virtual) proliferate for a fee? , inquired an entrepreneurial kibitzer friend. This is what a crapshoot Vitamanti was referring.

Thus, unless there is sameness in the syllabus, materials or courseware, methodology becomes elusive; methodology is probably the hardest to replicate in regard to "uniformity" because this relates to a living human being, a.k.a. the Teacher.

Every teacher is unique; no two teachers teach alike. There are a myriad approaches and methodologies – also the most difficult to "standardize." Materials or courseware or tests are reproducible in a cinch available online; not of course, how a teacher teaches.

Teachers will always bring different lesson perspectives into class and will likely emphasize different things. One sociology teacher for instance may stress familial context, while another on ethnocentricity. This is probably where the oft-quoted "academic freedom" is wonkily anchored, quips an apolitical activist kibitzer friend.

Teachers are expected to develop, collect, and construct their own tests. Since a test should measure what is taught, would you expect that a student could do equally well if he took a test, in the same unit, from all the teachers? The retired teacher from California inquired.

The rub is many teachers are unfamiliar with *valid test construction*; some would even modify well-established test construction rules. A case in point: a former teaching colleague of my kibitzer friend once prepared a matching-type examination with 40-items to match!

Many probably understand the concept of *item analysis* in test preparation so we are told, but despite of this would rather adopt online sources due to ease of availability and other often inexplicable reasons.

Basic

Studies indicate that it is valid or tolerable to declare it feasible to construct decent standardized-national tests for the lower elementary students where they are mostly concerned with the basics of reading, writing and arithmetic.

Empirical studies also suggest that as adolescent students mature, their ability to think and make decisions becomes more developed and more complex particularly during the tertiary or university phase. Cognitive development is ultimately heightened during adolescence.

Vitamanti averred that since state and national tests in the United States of America do not stress concepts, they tend to be rigid; therefore, in order for their students to do well, teachers will be forced to teach to the test.

The result is a watered-down education and students with rigid minds?

Now *we* know…

Psychology of death

By: Dr. Aggie Carson-Arenas
Columnist, Inquirer, US Bureau, October 21, 2021

"No one believes in his own death. In the *unconscious* everyone is convinced of his immortality," declared Sigmund Freud, the father of psychotherapy.

This is (perhaps) the fundamental reason theology, philosophy and science have such diverse concepts of death—from the most mystical, bizarre and to the most fanciful.

"The body is united by the soul; a sign of which is that, when the soul departs, the body is dissolved," wrote St. Aquinas in the *Summa contra Gentiles* seven-and-a-half-centuries ago.

Interpreting death has run the whole gamut of notion from a mere natural fact, pertaining to an organic matter, to the idea that death is the *telos* or "ultimate aim" of life, as a distinguishing feature of human existence, according to Marcuse, H., a German philosopher.

The *Black's Law Dictionary*, the most widely used law dictionary in the US first published 130 years ago, simply presents the traditional definition, "… stoppage of the circulation of the blood, and a cessation of the animal's vital functions, such as respiration and pulsation."

Death simply means the stoppage of heartbeat and breathing, which for centuries had been the criteria in declaring death. Experts had dubbed this *stoppage* as "clinical or circulatory death." No heartbeat or breath means simply you are dead, quipped a churlish kibitzer friend.

Concept

Technically, *clinical* or *circulatory* death means our body-cells or systems stop receiving oxygen and nutrients until unable to eliminate waste. However, few organs "survive" a bit longer—the heart for 15 minutes, the liver and kidney around an hour, the skin two hours, and the intestine more than three hours.

The brain's normal functionality can survive for only a few minutes before *irreversible damage* to the brain cells or neurons occurs.

"Despite its frequent use, the term 'clinical death' does not actually have a consistent meaning. In most hospitals, the doctor in charge of a patient's care makes the death determination….," according to Dr. Bernat, J., a neurologist now at Dartmouth-Hitchcock Medical Center, in New Hampshire.

Dr. Bernat bluntly clarified in an interview, "You are dead when a doctor says you are dead." There is the rub, retorted the churlish kibitzer.

Nevertheless, the dawn of sophisticated *resuscitating instrumentation* — in addition to the *innate expertise* of a doctor in declaring death seem to be redefining the meaning or determination of death, quipped my anti-iatrogenic-advocate kibitzer friend.

How many times have we heard of a "dead body" revived without any collateral damage to the body so long as the brain has not been deprived of blood for more than two or three minutes. Or a woman who gave birth to a baby three months after she *technically died*, reported Ghose, T., in her 2014 science article.

Guideline

The New York Department of Health (NYDH) first issued a guideline for determining "brain dead" (another way of identifying death) in 2005.

NYDH defines *brain death* as the irreversible loss of all function of the brain, including the brain stem. Three essential findings are involved: coma, absence of brain stem reflexes, and apnea.

The diagnosis of brain death is primarily clinical; the guideline hopes not only to educate health care providers regarding such determinations, but also to increase the public's confidence that such determinations are made through earnest evaluation in accordance with accepted medical standards, according to the report.

A patient properly determined to be *brain dead* is legally and clinically dead, so we are told. This is where the more sensitive and sophisticated instrumentations come in, quipped a techno-savvy kibitzer friend.

Many contemporary doctors equate death in term of a *complete brain wave activity cessation.* "No brain activity simply means death," according to Dr. Beacher of the Harvard Medical School. Today, this is verifiable by recording the *electrical activity* of the brain and interpreting "brain wave" data using an electroencephalograph (EEG) apparatus.

When the EEG displays a continuous straight line and sound on a monitor—commonly depicted theatrically in dramatic movies— known as *isoelectric flat line,* the patient is declared medically dead or brain dead.

However, a study in 2013 that suggested, "The brain may survive in deeper states of coma than the ones found during the isoelectric line." This study was led by Dr. Amzica, F., a neurophysiologist at Université de Montreal.

"Everybody thinks that the 'flat line' is the ultimate frontier of living brain," according to Dr. Amzica, who suspects the specific waves have *not* been discovered, simply because no one has bothered to look. Or (maybe) a more sensitive instrumentation for this remain elusive, quipped a kibitzer friend.

This extremely reductionist notion brought forth by Dr. Amzica's study seems to highlight the concept, "... *absence of evidence is not evidence of absence*," proposed by Drs. Altman, D. G. and Bland, J. M. This complicates the meaning of death some more.

"Some patients now considered to be in a persistent vegetative state might instead be considered dead. Nevertheless, because some people considered vegetative *show flickers of consciousness*, death certificates should only be issued when someone has met the criteria for brain death," according Dr. Whetstine, L., a philosopher at Walsh University in Ohio who studies death.

"Death should be defined as the irreversible *loss of that consciousness*," Dr. Whetstine concluded. Would an AI-technology (perhaps) enable scientists to precisely "quantify" consciousness during death?, quipped a thanatophobia-kibitzer friend.

Reality

Empirical studies indicate that dying today is a ghastly life episode. Complicated a million-fold by the pandemic.

A dying human feels more desolate, who is attached *literally* to myriad and expensive instrumentation; it is costly and highly dehumanized. To add insult to injury sometimes, ascertaining technically the exact time of death is mere conjecture.

Statistics show that humans rarely die because of old age per se. Death invariably follows some ailments, accident, shock or strain, or by microorganisms like Covid, which the body is unable to overcome. Not very many die naturally.

Albeit the final irony in all of this is: man is (probably) the only animal who consciously knows he has to die, once wrote an alter-ego kibitzer friend.

Shame is a soul-eating emotion

By: Dr. Aggie Carson-Arenas
Columnist, Inquirer, US Bureau, December 09, 2021

Josel was a grade-three student in a special school for the gifted whose short-pants were pulled down by a teacher in front of his classmates for missing an assignment (!), a mother conveyed to an alter-ego kibitzer friend of mine a few decades ago.

This seemingly remote incident exemplifies a teacher lacking empathy towards his students. What *educational concept* was whirling around inside this teacher's head to act the way he did at that moment?

Josel appeared diffident, although he also showed effeminate quirks, was a soft-spoken but intelligent ten-year-old who was known by teachers to be often publicly teased by classmates as '*bakla*' (gay). Was this particular teacher attempting to teach Josel a "lesson"?

The teacher probably was applying – unbeknownst to him –his *own version* of "conversion therapy," which was at the time not yet a buzzword even in clinical psychology, quipped my anti-conversion therapy advocate kibitzer friend.

Luckily the teacher never knew Dr. Eugen Steinach, a Viennese endocrinologist who "transplanted" testicular chemicals from straight men into gay men in attempts to change their sexual orientation. Like "conversion therapy," it was eventually exposed as ineffective and often harmful.

This was indeed a psychoeducational milestone for Josel: he simply vanished from the special school for the gifted. This happened during a time, in a culture where retribution or demanding remorse for the teacher's behavior was a joke.

The repercussion of this seemingly innocuous act by a bad teacher is apparently an invisible trauma roiling so much shame inside Josel's psyche and perhaps beclouded his personhood for the rest of his life.

Glitch

Trauma is an emotional response to a *terrible* event; where immediately after, shock and denial are typical. Moreover, longer term reactions include unpredictable emotions, and even myriad physical symptoms like headaches or nausea, according to the American Psychological Association (APA).

APA however clarified that, while these feelings are normal, some people have difficulty moving on with their lives. Was the pants-dropping a "terrible" event for a ten-year-old boy, enabling him to move on with life without psychophysiological glitch?

Shame is a trauma-related emotion, which according to the APA is a highly unpleasant self-conscious emotion arising from the sense of there being something dishonorable, immodest, or indecorous in one's own conduct or *circumstances*. Shame can have a profound effect on psychological adjustment and interpersonal relationships, added the APA.

Many studies consistently reveal a relationship between proneness to shame and a host of psychological symptoms, including depression, anxiety, eating disorders, subclinical sociopathy, and low *self-esteem*, so we are told.

Terrible

Josel's academic performance was probably the initial omen for this "terrible" event.

The term "terrible" in the definition presented by the APA seems arbitrary and vague, quipped my neurotic-lexiconic kibitzer friend. Losing a single toy-marble among 100 for a kid can be "terrible," yet *not* for another, added this kibitzer friend.

Drs. V. Felitti and R. Anda in 1995 somehow seem to have resolved this in coining *Adverse Childhood Experiences* (ACES); "adverse" is almost the twin-sister "terrible," quipped another lexiconic kibitzer friend. ACE encompasses the chronic, unpredictable, and stress-inducing events that some children face growing up, including enduring *chronic humiliation* that breeds shame.

Studies reveal that experiencing chronic, unpredictable stress like shame during childhood predisposes children to a constellation of chronic psychophysiological conditions in adulthood.

Detrimental

Contemporary studies, therefore, succinctly suggest that shame is detrimental to a youth's psychophysiological health. Moreover, studies indicate that women and younger people are the most likely to struggle with this emotion; what more with a transitioning gender, quipped an LBTQ advocate kibitzer friend.

Other studies also indicate that constantly feeling shame or being constantly inundated with shame is a link to *low self-esteem*. This is the self-approximation that something is wrong inside oneself, quipped another kibitzer friend.

This is the fundamental reason shame is particularly difficult to overcome, "It causes people to feel as if they are flawed at their core," wrote Dr. J. P. Tangney, a professor of psychology at George Mason

University in her book, "*Shame and Guilt: Emotions and Social Behavior*."

This means that "…with shame, you think, I am bad," internally cueing one that having a tainted or imperfect or checkered character or constitution feels a lot harder to change, so it causes the individual to isolate and withdraw, paraphrasing the context of Dr. J. P. Tangney's point. Was this the emotion Joel felt?

Culture

More than half a century ago, Drs. Guthrie, G. M. and Jacobs, P.J. wrote that shame or *hiya* sometimes develops from early childhood mainly through the subtle use of "*biro*" (teasing) by parents, siblings and other relatives to which children are subjected.

"One is teased about something about which one is known to be vulnerable, about which one is believed to be touchy," again according to Drs. Guthrie and Jacobs. They added that shame develops from early childhood mainly through constant teasing by parents, siblings and other relatives.

How many of us are guilty of fondly calling a child "*tabachuching*" (fatso)? Or making seemingly harmless joke or remark like, "dude, you have 'man boobs'" or "girl, you are as flat as a pancake," addressed especially to adolescents with such "obvious issues."

If only these youths can quantify the psychophysiological effects of these jokes or remarks with their *wearable* soon enough, conversion to psychosomatic symptoms might dissipate, quipped an Apple-wearable fanatic kibitzer friend.

Positive

Comparable with other traits, *hiya* or shame has positive effect, which helps maintain interpersonal relationships and keeps family honor, according to a Filipino psychologist Dr. M.S. Katigbak as early as 1966.

Studies show that Philippine society still upholds the value of "hiya" and puts the most onerous burden on a female adolescents than on males, according to Dr. Cruz, G. T., et al.. A premarital pregnancy for instance, is more likely to bring shame or loss of face on the female's family.

Nevertheless, contemporary studies also suggest that shame "play(s) a more positive adaptive function by regulating experiences of excessive and inappropriate interest and excitement and by diffusing potentially threatening social behavior," according to APA.

Hiya makes people employ the greatest kindness and politeness, wrote another Filipino author Dr. Senden almost half a century ago. This probably is what APA meant by "… diffusing potentially threatening social behavior."

Finally, Dr. Carl Gustav Jung founder of the psychoanalytic psychology truly aptly wrote: "Shame is a soul eating emotion."

My apology to Dr. Carl Gustav Jung for using his words for the title.

Thanks for bridging thoughts….

OTHER BOOKS BY DR. AGGIE CARSON-ARENAS

You're Okay, I am Perfect
(How teens, adolescents and those in between Quest for identity),
2021, with Abbygale Williamson Arenas-de Leon.

Bridging Thoughts Volume II
A compilation of psychology related published articles imbued
with Filipino contexts, 2020.

Understanding the Self (*Pag-unawa sa Sarili*) Through the Eye of
Adolescence), 2018.

Introduction to Psychology
(Understanding human behaviors), second edition, 2019.

Bridging Thoughts Volume, I
A collection of published articles on Philippine education,
psychology and other ephemera, 2018.

Secrets of Practical Hypnosis
(Introductory manual to hypnotherapy, illustrated), 2010, with
Allen-Chriss Williamson Arenas.

ABOUT THE AUTHOR

Dr. Aggie Carson-Arenas is a Certified Clinical Psychology Specialist, a former associate professor and university research director. He is a Behavior Analyst Specialist in Nevada, an educator, clinician, researcher, consultant, columnist, and a published author. He has a doctorate in Education, a master's degree in Guidance and Counseling, and attended a second doctorate in Clinical Psychology at the University of the Philippines. Dr. Carson-Arenas is a Fellow and a former Board Member of the Psychological Association of the Philippines (PAP), and a member of the American Psychological Association (APA). Dr. Carson-Arenas is based and quasi-retired in Las Vegas, Nevada with his perfect-wife Aida. They have four children, Abbygale, Ann-Marie, Allen-Chriss and Arlee-John; five grandsons, Amer, Ijah, Adrian, Eli, Ethan and a granddaughter, Ann-Jayleen; and four home-friends, a rabbit named Johnny, Bruskah a desert turtle with two other tiny ones, Luxor and Bally.

Made in the USA
Las Vegas, NV
05 December 2023

82135922R00090